The Charm of
The English
Garden

The Charm of
The English
Garden

Dion Clayton Calthrop

with 32 full-colour illustrations by
BEATRICE PARSONS, GEORGE ELGOOD
and others

Bracken Books
LONDON

Originally published in 1910 as *The Charm of Gardens* by Adam & Charles Black.

This edition published 1985 by Bracken Books,
a division of Bestseller Publications Ltd,
Brent House, 24 Friern Park, North Finchley,
London N12, England.

ISBN 0 946495 57 2

Printed and bound by Kultura, Hungary.

CONTENTS

PART I

A VIEW OF ENGLAND

PART II

GARDENS AND HISTORY

CONTENTS

PART III

PART IV

GARDEN MOODS

LIST OF ILLUSTRATIONS

Between pages 32 and 33

PART I

A VIEW OF ENGLAND

I

THE SPIRIT OF GARDENS

ONCE, I remember well, when I was hungering for a breath of country air, a woman, brown with the caresses of the wind and sun, brought the Spring to my door and sold it to me for a penny. The husky rough scent of those Primroses gave me news of England that I longed to hear. When I had placed my flowers in a bowl and put them on the table where I worked, they told me stories of the lanes and woods, how thrushes sang, and the wild Cherry Blossom flared delicately across the purpling trees.

A flower often will reclaim a mood when nothing else will bring it back.

To garden, to garner up the seasons in a little space, is part of every wise man's philosophy. To sow the seeds, to watch the tender shoots come out and brave the light and rain, to see the buds lift up their heads, and then to catch one's breath as the flowers open and display their precious colours, living, breathing jewels, is enough to live for. But there is more than that. A man may choose the feast to spread before his eyes, may sow old memories and see them grow, and feel the answering colours in his heart. This Rose he used to pass on his way to school ; it nodded to him over the high red wall, while next to it a Purple Clematis clung, arching over, so that, by standing on his pile of school-books, he could reach the flowers. This patch of Golden

3

Marigolds reminds him of a long border in the garden where he spent his boyhood (they used to grow behind the bee skeps, had a little place to themselves next to the Horseradish and the early Lettuces). There's a hedge of Lavender full of association, he may remember how he was allowed (or was it set him for a task ?) to cut great sheaves of it and take them to the Apple-room, and hang them up to dry over old newspapers. To look at Lavender brings back the curious musty smell of that store-room, where Apples wintered on long shelves ; where the lawn-mower stood, and the brooms, and the scythe (to cut the orchard grass), and untidy bundles of bass hung with string and coils of wire. What a wonderful place that store-room was, with the broken door and the rusty lock that creaked as the big key turned to let him in : to reach the latch he had to stand on tip-toe, and to turn the key seemed quite a grown-up task. There was all a garden needs stored in that room. It had been a dining-room once, a hundred years ago, a room where the members of a bowling club convivially met and fought old games ; bias, twist, jack, all the terms ring in his ears, even the click of the bowls, sharp on the summer air, comes back ; and the plastered ornamental ceiling had sagged and dropped away here and there, showing the laths. There was a big dusty window, across which the twisted arms of a Wisteria stretched, and a broken window seat in it that opened like a box to hold the bowls. Just the hedge of Lavender brings back the picture of the boy whose cherished dreams hung about those four walls ; who, having strung his bunches, neatly tied, on wooden pegs along the walls, and spread his papers underneath to catch the falling seeds, sat, book in hand, and travelled into foreign lands with Mungo Park. There, on his left, and facing him as well, shelves lined the walls, and Pears,

4

Apples and Medlars were arranged in rows, while by his side, placed on the window ledge to catch the sun, were fallen Nectarines, Peaches and big yellow Plums set to ripen.

What curious things a garden store-room holds ! The tins, slopped over, of weed-killer, of patent plant foods, of fine white sand. The twisted string, criss-crossed upon a peg of wood, covered with whitewash, the string that serves to guide the marker for the tennis-court. Then an array of nets to cover Currant bushes, and bid birds beware of Gooseberries, Cherries and ripe Strawberries. A barrow, full of odds and ends, baskets, queer little bags of seeds, a heap of Groundsel gathered for a bird and lying there forgotten. Like a Dutch picture, half in gloom with bright lights on the shears, and along the edge of the scythe, and on the curved wire mesh made to guard young seedlings. Empty seed packets on the floor, bright coloured pictures of the flowers on the outsides, a little soiled by the earth and the gardener's thumb.

Plant memories, indeed ! A man may plant a host of them and never then recapture all his joys. There's his first love garnishing a rustic arch, a deep yellow Rose, beautiful in the bud—William Allen Richardson : she wore them in her sash. He can laugh now and see the long yellow hair floating in a cloud behind her as she ran, and the twinkling black legs, and the merry pretty face looking down on him from between the leaves of the Apple-tree she climbed. He grows that Apple in his orchard now, and toasts her memory when the first ripe fruit of it shines on the dish before him at dessert.

The Clove Carnation with its spice-like scent he bought from a barrow in a London slum, brought with care—wrapped in paper on the rack of the railway carriage—and planted it here. This Picotee he hailed with joy

5

in the flower-market at Saint Malo and carried it across the sea, each bloom tied up to a friendly length of cane. His neighbours marvel at his pains, but it recalls many a happy day to him.

There, in a corner under a nut-tree, is a grass bank thick with Primrose plants—another memory. A picture comes to him from the Primroses very clear, very distinct, a picture of the world gone black, of a day when a boy thought heaven and earth purposeless, cruel; when he ran from a garden to the woods and threw himself on a bank, covered with Primroses, sobbing and weeping till the world was blotted out with his tears, because his dog had died. It had been the first thing he had learnt to love, the first thing he had had to care for, to look after. All his childish ideas were whispered into the big retriever's silky coat. They had secret understandings, a different language, ideas in common, and the dog's death was his first hint of death in the world. Years after, when he planted this garden, he gave a place to Don, and planted the Primroses himself. The earth was kindly and the flowers flourished. The earth is kindly, even your cynic knows that and marks the spot where he hopes to lie, and thinks, not sourly, of the Daisies over his head.

There is something more than memory in a garden. There is that urgent need man has to be part of growing life. He must have open spaces, he takes health from the sight of a tree in bud, from the sight of a newly ploughed field, from a plant or so in a window-box, a flower in his button-hole. Men, who by a thousand ties are held at desks in cities, look up and hear a caged thrush sing, and their thoughts fly out to fields and the common wayside flowers, and, for a moment, the offices are filled with the perfume—indescribable—of the open road.

THE SPIRIT OF GARDENS

There is that in the hum and business of a garden that makes for peace ; the senses are softly stirred even as the heart finds wings. No greeting is as sweet as the drowsy murmur of bees, in garden, lane or open heath. No day so good as that which breaks to song of birds. No sight so happy as the elegant confusion of flower border still wet and glistening with the morning dew.

I heard a man once deliver a learned lecture on the Persian character, full of history, romance and thoughtful ideas. Towards the end of his discourse I began to feel that he, indeed, knew the Persian inside out, but that I could catch but a fleeting and momentary glimpse of his knowledge. Then, by way of background to an anecdote, he mirrored, with loving care and wealth of detail, Oriental in its imagery and elaboration, the gardens in a palace. There was a stream of clear water running through the garden, and the owner had paved the bed of the stream with exquisite old tiles ; white Irises bloomed along the banks, white Roses, growing thickly, dropped scented petals in the stream. I have as good as lived in that garden ; I saw it so well, and what little I know of the Persian I know from that description. Omar is more than a dead poet to me now ; I can smell the Roses blooming over his grave.

There should be a sundial in every garden to mark the true beginning and the end of day ; some noise of water somewhere ; bees ; good trees to give shade to us and shelter to the birds ; a garden-house with proper amount of flower-lore on shelves within ; a walk for scent alone, flowers grown perfume-wise ; a solitary place, if possible, where should be a nest of owls ; a spread of lawn to rest the eyes, no cut beds in it to spoil the symmetry, and at least one border for herbaceous plants. If this is greedy of good things leave out the owls—that's but a fanciful thought. Do you know

7

what a small space this requires ? Those who might be
free and yet choose to live in towns might have it all
for the price of the rent of the ground their kitchen
covers.

There are those aching spirits to whom no land is
home, whose feet go wandering over the world ; gipsy-
spirits searching one must suppose for peace of mind
in constant new sights. For them the well-ordered
garden with its high walls, its neat lawn, its fair carriage-
drive, is but a dull prison-house, and even if in the course
of their wanderings they stray into such a place their
talk is all of other lands ; of scarlet twisted flowers in
Cashmere ; of fields of Arum Lilies near Table Mountain ;
of the sad-grey Olives and the gorgeous Orange groves
of Spain ; the Poppy fields of China, or the brightly
painted Tulips growing orderly in Holland. We with
our ancestral rookery near by, our talk of last year's
nests, or overweening pride in the soft snows of Mrs.
Simpkin's Pinks, seem to these folk like prisoners, who
having tamed a mouse proclaim it chief of all the
animal world. But ask of the Garden of England and
the flowers it affords and see their eyes take on a far-
away look as the road calls to them, and hear them at
their own lore of roadside flowers, praising and loving
Traveller's Joy, the gilt array of Buttercups, the dusty
pink of Ragged Robin, and the like sweet joys the vaga-
bond holds dear. This one can whistle like a blackbird ;
that one has boiled the roots of Dandelions (Dent de Lion,
a charming name) and has been cured by their juices.
He knows that if he sees the delicate parachutes of
Dandelion, Coltsfoot, or of Thistle-fly when there is not
a breath of wind, then there will be rain. They read
the skies, hear voices in the wind, take courses from the
stars, and know the time of day from flowers. These
men, having none of the spirit that inspires your gar-

8

dener, see the results of the work and smile pleasantly, ask, perhaps, the name of some flower, to please you, know something of soils, praise your Mulberries, and admire your collection of Violas, but soon they are off and away, breathing more freely for leaving the sheltered peace of your well-kept place, and vanish to Spitzbergen or the Chinese desert in search of what their souls crave. We are different ; we sit in the cool of the evening, overlooking our sweet-scented borders, gaining joy from the gathering night that paints out the detail of our world, and hope quietly for a soft, gentle rain in the night to stiffen the flowers' drooping heads. We English are gardeners by nature : perhaps the greyness of our skies accounts for our desire to make our gardens blaze with colours.

We have our memories, our desire for peace, our love of colour, and, at the back of all, something infinitely more grand.

> " No lily muffled hum of a summer bee
> But finds some coupling with the spinning stars ;
> No pebble at your foot, but proves a sphere ;
> . . . Earth's crammed with heaven,
> And every common bush afire with God :
> But only he who knows takes off his shoes."

II

THE GARDEN OF ENGLAND: THE PATCHWORK QUILT

EVEN your most unadventurous fellow can hardly look on a fair prospect of fields and meadows, woods, villages with smoking chimneys, a river, and a road, without a certain feeling rising in him that he would like to tread the road that winds so dapperly through the country, and discover for himself where it leads.

To those who love their country the road is but a garden path running between borders of fair flowers whose names and virtues should be known to every child.

A poet can weave a story from the speck of mud on a fellow traveller's boot—the red soil of a Devonshire lane calls up such pictures of fern-covered banks, such rushing streams, as make a poem in themselves.

It strikes one from the very first how neatly most of England is kept. The dip and rise of softly swelling hills across which the curling ribbon of the road winds leisurely between neat hedges, the fields in patches, coloured brown and green, golden with Corn, scarlet with Poppies, yellow with Buttercups; the circular bunches of trees under whose shade fat cattle stand lazily switching their tails at flies; the woods, hangers, shaws and coppices, glades, dells, dingles and combes, all set out so orderly and precise that, from a hill, the country has the appearance of a patchwork quilt set in

THE GARDEN OF ENGLAND

a pleasant irregularity, studded with straggling farms, and little sleepy villages where the resonant note of the church clock checks off the drowsy hours. The road that runs through this quilt land seems like a thread on which villages and market towns are strung, beads of endless variety, some huddled in a bunch upon a hill, some long and straggling, some thatched and warm, red-bricked and creeper-covered, others white with roofs of purple slate, others of grey stone, others of warm yellow. All alive with birds and flowers and village children, butterflies and trees; fed by broad rivers, or hanging over singing streams or deep in the lush grass of water meadows gay with kingcups.

This garden is for us who care to know it. We can take the road, our garden path, and pluck, as we will, flowers of all kinds from our borders; sleep in our garden on beds of bracken pulled and piled high under trees; or on soft heaps of heather heaped under sheltering stones. If we know our garden well enough it will give us food—salads, fruits and nuts; it will cure us of our ills by its herbs; feed our imagination by the quaint names of flower and herb. Here's a small list that will sing a man to sleep, dreaming of England.

Poet's Asphodel.	Celandine.
Shepherd's Purse.	Columbine.
Our Lady's Bedstraw.	Adder's Tongue.
Water Soldier.	Speedwell.
Rowan.	Thorn Apple.
Hound's Tongue.	Virgin Bower.
Gipsy Rose.	Whin.
Fool's Parsley.	

These alone of hundreds give a lift to the day : there's a story to each of them.

Take our England as a garden and let the eye roam over the land. Here's the flat country of the Fens,

11

long, long vistas of fields, with spires and towers sticking up against the sky. Plenty of rare flowers there for your gardener, marsh flowers, water plants galore. That's the place to see the sky, to watch a summer storm across the plain, to see the Poplars bending in an angry wind, and the white windmills glare against purple rain clouds. Few hedges here but plenty of banks and dykes, and canals they call drains. Here you may find Marsh Valerian, Water Crowsfoot, Frogbit, pink Cuckoo-flowers, Bog Bean, Sundews, Sea Lavender, and Bladder-worts. The Sundews alone will give you an hour's pleasure with their glistening red glands tricked out to catch unwary flies and midges.

Then there's a wild garden waiting you by stone walls in the dales of Derbyshire, or in the Yorkshire wolds, or the Lancashire fells. On the open heaths, where the grey roads wind through warm carpets of ling and heather, you can fill your nostrils with the sweet scent of Gorse and Thyme.

I was sitting one hot afternoon, drawing the twisted bole of a Beech tree. All the wood in which I sat was stirring with life ; the dingle below me a mist of flowers, Primroses, Wind-flowers, Hyacinths whose bells made the air softly fragrant. Above me the sky showed through a trellis-work of young leaves, the distance of the wood was purple with opening buds, and the floor was a swaying sea of Bluebells dancing in a gentle breeze. Squirrels chattered in the trees ; now and then a wood pigeon flopped out of a tree, and a blackbird whistled in some hidden place.

All absorbed in my work, following the grotesquely beautiful curves of the beech roots, I heard no sound of approaching footsteps. A voice behind me said "Good," and I started, dropping my pencil in my confusion.

12

"Sorry. Didn't mean to startle you," said the voice.

I turned round and saw a man standing behind me, a man without a cap, with curly brown hair, and a face coloured deep brown by the sun. He was dressed in a faded suit of greenish tweed, wore a blue flannel shirt, carried a thick stick in his hand, and had a worn-looking box slung over his shoulders by a stained leather strap.

I suppose my surprise showed in my face in some comic way, for he laughed heartily, showing a set of strong white teeth.

"No, I'm not Pan," he said laughing, " or a keeper, or a vision. I'm a gardener."

His admirable assurance and pleasant address were very captivating.

I asked him what he did there, and he immediately sat down by me, pulled out a black clay pipe, and lit up before replying. He extended the honours of his match to my cigarette and I noticed that his hands were well formed, and that he wore a silver ring on the little finger of his right hand.

When he had arranged himself to his comfort, propping his back against a tree and crossing his legs, he told me he was a gardener on a very large scale.

I wished him joy of his garden, at which he smiled broadly, and informed me in the most matter-of-fact way that he gardened the whole of Great Britain.

For a moment I wondered if I had fallen in with an amiable lunatic, but a closer inspection of his face showed me he was sane, uncommonly healthy, and, I judged, a clever man.

"A vast garden ? " I said.

Without exactly replying to my remark, which was put half in the manner of a question, he said, partly to himself, " The slight fingers of April. Do you notice how delicate everything is ? "

I had noticed. The air was full of suggestion, the flowers were very fairylike, the green of the trees very tender.

" Pied April," said I.

Instead of answering me again he unstrapped the box that now lay beside him on the grass, opened it and took from it a beautiful Fritillaria.

" There's one of the April Princesses, if you like," he said. " There are not many about here, just an odd one or two ; plenty near Oxford though."

" You know Oxford ? " said I.

" Guess again," he said, smiling. " I'm no Oxford man, but I know the woods about there well. Please go on working ; I'll talk."

I was about to look at my watch when he stopped me.

" It's half-past two," he said. " The slant of the sun on the leaves ought to tell you that."

I was amused, interested in the man ; he was so odd and quaint. " I've not eaten my lunch yet," I said. " Perhaps you'll share it with me."

" I was wondering if you'd invite me," he replied. " I'm rather hungry."

I had, luckily, enough for two. Slices of ham, some cheese, a loaf of new bread, and a full flask. Very soon we were eating together like old friends.

In an inconsequent way he asked me what I thought of the name of Noakes.

I said it was as good as any other.

" Let's have it Noakes, then," he said, laughing again. A very merry man.

" About this garden of yours, Mr. Noakes ? " I asked.

He tapped his wooden box and said, " If you want to

know, I'm a herbalist. You can scarcely call me a civilised being, except on occasions when I do go among my fellow men to winter." He pulled a cap and a pair of gloves out of his pocket. " My titles to respectability," he said.

" And in the Spring ? "

" I take to the road with the Coltsfoot and the Butter-burrs. I come out with the first Violet, and the Pussy-cat Willow. I wander, all through the year, up and down the length and breadth of England, with my box of herbs. I get my bread and cheese that way—while you draw for pleasure."

" Partly."

" It must be for pleasure, or you wouldn't take so much pains. I suppose you think I'm a very disgraceful person, a bad citizen, a worse patriot. But I know the news of the world better than those who read newspapers. Although I trade on superstitions, I do no harm."

" Do you sell your herbs ? "

" Colchicum for gout—Autumn Crocus, you know it," he replied. " Willow-bark quinine ; Violet distilled, for coughs. Not a bad trade—besides, it keeps me free."

I hazarded a question. " Tell me—you must observe these things—do swifts drink as they fly ? It has often puzzled me."

" I don't know," said he. " Ask Mother Nature. Some of these things are the province of professors. I'm not a learned man ; just a herbalist."

At that moment a thrush began to sing in a tree overhead. My friend cocked his head, just like an animal.

" There's the wise thrush," he quoted softly, " he sings his song twice over."

15

THE CHARM OF GARDENS

" So you read Browning," I said.

" I have a garret and a library," he said. " Winter quarters. We shall meet one day, and you'll be surprised. I actually possess two dress suits. It's a mad world." He stopped abruptly to listen to the thrush. " This is better than the Carlton or Delmonico's, anyhow ! "

" What do you do ? " I asked. " Go from village to village selling herbs ? "

" That's about it. Lord ! Listen to that bird. I heard and saw a nightingale sing once in a shaw near Ewelme. I think a thrush is the better musician, though. Yes, I sell my herbs, all sorts and kinds. Drugs and ointments, very simple I assure you—Hemlock and Poppy to cure the toothache. Wood Sorrel—full of oxalic acid, you know, like Rhubarb—for fevers. Aconite for rheumatics—very popular medicine I make of that, sells like hot cakes in water meadow land, so does Agrimony for Fen ague. Tansy and Camomile for liver —excellent. Hellebore for blisters, and Cowslip pips for measles—I'm a regular quack, you see."

" And it's worth doing, is it ? "

He leaned back, his pipe between his lips, a very contented man. " Worth doing ! " he said. " Worth owning England, with all the wonderful mornings, and the clean air ; worth waking up to the scent of Violets ; worth lying on your back near a Bean field on a summer day ; worth seeing the Bracken fronds uncurl ; watching kingfishers ; worth having the fields and hedgerows for a garden, full of flowers always—I should think so. I earn my bread, and I'm happy, far happier than most men. I can lend a hand at haymaking, at the harvest ; at sheep-shearing, at the cider press, at hoeing, when I'm tired of my own company. I've worked the seines in the mackerel season on the South coast—do you know the bend of shore by Lyme and Charmouth ?

16

I've ploughed in the Lowlands, and found lost sheep in the Lake Country ; caught moles for a living in Norfolk, and cut Hop-poles in Kent, and Heather in the Highlands. —And I'm not forty, and I'm never ill."

" It sounds delightful."

He rose to his feet and gave me his hand.

" We shall meet again," he said laughing. " Perhaps in the conventional armour of starched shirts and inky black. For the present—to my work," he pointed over his shoulder. " I'm building hen-coops for a widow. *Hasta luego.*"

With that he vanished as quietly as he came. Almost as soon as the trees had hidden him from my sight, a blackbird began to whistle, then stopped, and a laugh came out of the woods.

Altogether a very strange man.

I found, when he had gone, that he had written something on a piece of paper and had pinned it to the tree with a long thorn. It was this :

" I think, very likely, you may not know Ben Jonson's ' Gipsy Benediction.' If you don't, accept the offering as a return for my excellent lunch.

"The faerybeam upon you—
    The stars to glisten on you—
        A moon of light
        In the noon of night,
    Till the firedrake hath o'er gone you !
    The wheel of fortune guide you ;
    The boy with the bow beside you ;
        Run aye in the way
        Till the bird of day,
    And the luckier lot, betide you."

He signed, at the foot, " Noakes, Under the Greenwood Tree." And he seemed to have written some of his clear laughter into it.

17

III

A COUNTRY LANE: A MEMORY
FROM ABROAD

I was looking at a vision of the world upside down,
mirrored in the deep blue of a still sea. Where the
inverted picture of my boat gleamed white, and the
rope that moored her to a tree showed grey, I saw the
dark fir trees growing upside down, the bank of emerald
grass looking more brilliant because of the grey-green
lichened rocks ; a black rock, glistening, hung with
brown seaweed, made the vision clear, and, over all,
clouds chased each other in the sky, seemingly below
me. They were those round fleecy clouds, like sheep,
and they reminded me of something I could not quite
arrest.

A fish swam—dash—across my mirror, another and
another, rippling the sky, the trees, the bank, distorting
everything. Then I looked up and saw a fishing-
boat come sailing by with its great orange and
tawny sails all set out to catch the land breeze ; and
bright blue nets hung out ready, floating and billowing
in the slight wind. There was a creaking of ropes
and a hum of Breton as the sailors talked. From my
moorings by the island I watched her sail—*Saint Nicholas*
she was called, and had a little figure of the Madonna
on her stern. Out of the land-locked harbour she
slipped, tacking to make the neck that led to the outer
harbour, and there she was going to meet other gaily

18

coloured ships and sail with them to the sardine grounds off the coast of Spain.

After she had passed, leaving her wide white wake in the still waters, I followed her in my mind, seeing the nets cast and the shimmering silver fish drawn up, and the long loaves of bread eaten, with wine and onions, until the waters round me were quiet again, and I could look once more into my mirror and wonder what it was the flocks of clouds said to my brain.

It came in a flash. Big Claus said to Little Claus, " After I threw you into the river in the sack, where did you get all those sheep and cattle ? " And Little Claus said, " Out of the river, brother, for there I came upon a man in beautiful meadows, and he was tending the sheep and cattle. There were so many that he gave me a flock of sheep and a herd of cattle for myself, and I drove them out of the river and up here to graze." Now they were looking over the bridge at the time, and the description Little Claus gave of the meadows and the sheep below in the river made the mouth of Big Claus begin to water with greed. As they looked, Little Claus pointed excitedly at the water, and said, " Look, brother, there go a flock of sheep under your very nose." It was, really, nothing but the reflection of the clouds in the water, but Big Claus was too interested to think of this, and he implored his brother to tie him in a sack and push him into the water, that he, too, might get some of these wonderful herds. This Little Claus did, and that was the end of Big Claus.

How well I remember now—so well that when I looked into the water and saw the fleecy clouds go floating by, the picture changed for me and I saw an English country lane, and a small boy sitting under a hedge out of a summer shower, and he was deep in

19

dreams over an old brown volume of " Grimm's Fairy Tales."

How wonderful the lane smelt after the rain ! The Honeysuckle filled the air and mingled with the smell of warm wet earth. It was a deep lane, with the high hedges grown so rank and wild that they nearly crossed overhead, and the curved arms of the Dog Roses criss-crossed against the patch of turquoise sky. The thin new thread of a single wire crossed high overhead, shining like gold in the sun. It went, I knew, to the Coast Guard Station below me, and I remember clearly how I used to wonder what flashed across the wire to those fortunate men : news of thrilling wrecks, of smugglers creeping round the point, of battle-ships put out to sea, and other tales the sailors told me.

The lane was deep and twisted, and so narrow that when a flock of sheep was driven down it, the dogs ran across the backs of the sheep to head off stragglers. What a cloud of white dust they made, and how thick it lay on the leaves and flowers until the rain washed them clean again.

On the day of which I was dreaming, there had been one of those sharp angry storms, very short and fierce, with growling thunder in the distance, and purple and deep grey clouds flying along with torn, rust-coloured edges. I had sheltered under a quick-set hedge (set, that is, while the thorn was alive—quick, and bent into a kind of wattle pattern by men with sheepskin gloves) and where I sat, under a wayfaring tree (the Guelder Rose), the lane had a double turn, fore and aft, so that a space of it was quite shut off, like an island. I had my garden here and knew all the flowers and the butterflies.

On this day the rain washed the Foxgloves and made them gay and bright, each bell with a sparkling drop of water on its lips. The Brambles had long rows of drops on them, all shining like jewels, until a yellow-hammer perched on one of the arched sprays and shook all the raindrops off in a fluster of bright light

Behind me, and in front, trailing Black Bryony twisted its arms round Traveller's Joy, Honeysuckle and Wild Roses. Here and there, pink and white Bindweed hung, clinging to the hedge. By me, on the bank, Monkshood, Our Lady's Cushion, and Butterfly Orchis grew, all shining with the rain, and the Silverweed shone better than them all.

Presently came two great cart horses, their trappings jingling, down my lane, and on the back of one, riding sideways, a small boy, swaying as he rode. His face was a perfect country poem, blue eyes, shaded by a battered hat of felt, into the band of which a Dog Rose was stuck. His hair, like Corn, shone in the sun, and his face, red and freckled, a blue shirt, faded by many washings and sun-bleached to a fine colour, thick boots, a hard horny young fist, and in his mouth a long stem of feathery grass. He looked as much part of Nature as the flowers themselves. There was some sort of greeting as he passed. I can see the group now ; the slow patient horses, the boy, the yellow canvas coat slung to dry across the horse's neck, a straw basket, from which a bottle neck protruded, hitched on the horse's collar. They passed the bend in the lane and the boy began to whistle an aimless tune, but very good to hear. And it was England, every bit of it, the kind of thing one hungers for when a southern sun is beating pitilessly on one's head, or when the rains in the tropics bring out overpowering scents, heavy and stifling.

So I might have dreamed on about this garden lane

21

THE CHARM OF GARDENS

I carried in my mind, had not the tide turned and little waves begun to lop the sides of my boat.

I slipped my moorings, shipped the oars, and sailed home quietly on the tide under a clear blue sky from which all the clouds had vanished like my dream.

IV

FIELDS

A MAN will tell you how he has walked to such and such
a place "across the fields," with an air of saying,
" You, I suppose, not knowing the country, painfully
pursue the highroad." He has the look of one who
has made the discovery that it is good and wise to
leave the beaten track, the cart rut, and the plain
and obvious road, and has adventured in a daring
spirit from stile to stile, from gate to ditch, where only
the knowing ones may go. He is generally so occupied
in the pride of reaching his destination by these means,
that he has had little time to look about him and enjoy
the expanse of country. For all that, he is a man
after my own heart for, in a sense, he becomes part
owner of England with me as soon as he puts his leg
across a stile and begins to cast an eye across country.

There is an extraordinary satisfaction in following
a footpath, that is made doubly sweet if one sucks in
the joy of the day, and the blitheness of that through
which we pass. To be knee-high in a bean field in
flower is as good a thing as I know, more especially
if it be on a hillside overlooking the sea.

I sat once on the polished rail of a stile (very well
made with cross arms to hold by, like two short step-
ladders, each with one long arm) and looked at a path
I had taken that lay through a field of whispering oats.
They seemed to hold a thousand secrets that they passed

23

from ear to ear all down the field, and when the breeze
came, and blew birds across the hedge, the whole field
swayed, showing a rustling, silken surface, as if it
enjoyed a great joke. The Poppies and Cornflowers
and the White Convolvulus had no part in the conversation of the Oats, but field mice had, and ran across the
path hurrying like urgent messengers, and once a mole
nosed its way from the earth by my stile and vanished
grumbling—like some gruff old gentleman—along the
hedgerow. I never saw a field laugh as much as that
field, or be so frivolous, or so feminine. The field at
my back was more like a great lady in a green velvet
gown, embroidered with Daisies. There, at the bottom
of the field, was a pond like a bright blue eye in the
green, and lazy cattle, red and white, stood in it, while
others lay under a chestnut tree near by.

Down in the valley, a long undulating spread before
me, fields of different hues, some green, some brown,
some golden with ripe Corn, lay baked in the heat,
quivering under a calm blue sky. In one field a man
was sharpening a scythe with a whetstone—the rasp
came floating up to me clearly, and presently he began
to open a field of wheat for the reaping machine I could
see, with men round her, under a clump of trees. Next
to this field was a narrow strip of coarse grass all aglow
with Buttercups, then a wide triangular field, with a
pit in the corner of it, snowed over with Daisies, and
then a farm looking like a toy place, neat with white
painted railings, and a dovecote, and a long barn covered
over with yellow Stone Crop. I could see—all in
miniature—the farmer come out of his house door,
beckon to a dog, and walk past a row of Hollyhocks
and a flush of pink Sweet Williams, open the gate and
cross a road to the Corn-field. The dog leapt ahead of
him, barking joyously.

24

FIELDS

A little further down, and cut off partly from view by the May tree that sheltered me, was a village, white and grey, sheltered by Elm trees. In the midst of the handful of cottages the square-towered flint church stood with Ivy on the tower and dark Yews in the churchyard. The graves in the churchyard looked like the Daisies in the distant field, as if they grew there. At the back of the church, and facing the high road, was a line of trees from whence came an incessant noise of rooks.

Very few things moved on the high road, a lumbering waggon, the doctor's trap, a bicycle, and then the carrier's cart with a man I knew driving it, a very pleasant man who preached in the Sion Chapel on Sundays and chalked up texts in the tilt of his waggon —but with a shrewd eye to business : a man who never forgave a debt.

As I sat on my stile I felt this was all mine : no person there knew the beauty of it as I did, or cared to capture its sweetness as I did. No one but I saw the field of Oats laugh, or cared to note the business of the dragon fly, or the flashing patterns of the butterflies. I had seen these fields turned up, rich and brown, under the plough, and tender green when the seeds came up, and waving green, and gold when they bore their harvest of Corn, or silver and green with roots and red with Beets. I had counted the sheep on the hillsides, and watched the cattle stray in a long line to be milked at milking time, and though I did not farm an acre of it, I owned it with my heart, and gathered its harvest with my eyes.

Every field footpath had its story, the road was rich in old romance, and hidden by the trees at the head of the valley was the big house where my hostess lived and with a loving hand directed all this little world—but I doubt if she owned it more than I.

To end all this, comes a little maid through the Oats, almost hidden by them, her face quivering with tears because of a misplaced trust in a bunch of Nettles. So we apply Dock leaves and a penny, and a farthing's worth of country wisdom, and part friends—I to the head of the valley, she to her father's farm on the other side of the hill.

V

EPISODE OF THE CONTENTED TAILOR

NOT a hundred yards out of a certain village I came across a little man dressed in grey. We were alone on the road, we were going in the same direction, and I came to learn that he travelled with as little purpose as I.

As soon as I saw his face, his jaunty walk, his knapsack and his stick, I knew him for a friend.

I hailed him. He stopped, smiled pleasantly, and fell in with my stride. We soon found a mutual bond of esteem. It appeared we were out in search of adventures.

He explained to me, quite simply, that he was not going anywhere, and that he proposed to be some four months about it.

" Just walking about looking at things," he volunteered.

" That is my case," I replied.

" I'm a tailor, sir," said he.

" Having a look at the cut of the country ? "

He gave a little friendly nod.

" And do you tailor as you go along ? " I asked, for I had never met a travelling tailor before : tinkers galore ; haberdashers aplenty ; patent medicine men a few ; sailors ; old soldiers (the worst) ; apothecaries I have mentioned ; gentlemen, many ; ploughboys, purse thieves, one or two, and ugly customers—

they were in a dark lane—but a tailor, never. It seemed all the world could tread the high road but a tailor. Then I remembered my fairy tales—" Seven at a Blow "—and laughed aloud.

" I've given up my trade," he explained, as we began to mount the hill. " No more sitting on a bench for me in the spring or summer. I do a bit in the winter, but I'm a free man on two pounds ten a week."

And he was young—forty at the most.

" Put by ? " said I.

He smiled again. " Not quite, sir. I had a little bit put by, but a brother of mine went to Australia, and made a fortune—he died, poor Tom, and left his money to me and my sister. Two pound ten a week for each of us."

" And it has brought you—this," I explained, pointing with my stick at the expanse of country. " It's like a romance."

" Isn't it ? "

" Then you read romances ? " I asked quickly.

" I read all I can lay hands on," he replied. " I'm living just as my sister and I dreamed we'd live if ever something wonderful happened."

" And it has happened ? "

" You're right, sir. My sister lives in the little cottage I bought with my savings. She's got all she wants—all anybody might want, you might say. A cottage, six-roomed, all white, with a Pink Rose growing over the porch, and a canary in a cage in the parlour. Then there's a garden, and a bit of orchard, and bees and a river at the bottom of the little meadow, and a Catholic Church within a stone's throw—so it's all right. She's a rare good gardener, is my sister."

" I envy you both," I said.

He looked me up and down for a moment before

28

speaking. " No cause for you to do that, I expect, sir."

" Well, you know what you want, and you've got it."

We had reached the crest of the hill now after a longish climb. It was a hot day and I proposed a rest. Besides, it was one o'clock and I was hungry.

I had four hard boiled eggs, and he had bread and cheese—we divided our goods evenly, and ate comfortably under a hedge in a field.

" I've often sat on my bench," he said, " and looked out at the sun in the dusty street and wondered if I should ever be able to sit out in it on the grass and have nothing to do. We used to go for a day in the country, I and my sister, whenever I could spare the money, and it was a holiday. You wouldn't believe what the sight of green fields and trees meant to me and my sister : you see the hedgerows were the only garden we could afford, and we could ill-afford that. My sister used to talk about the Roses she'd have, and the Carnations, and the Sunflowers and Asters, when our ship came home. It came home—think of that." He stretched his limbs luxuriously. " And here we are with everything, and more."

" And more ? " I asked.

" Well, you see, it is more, somehow. I'm ' me ' now —do you follow the idea ? I never knew what it was to be on my own : just ' me.' I can lie abed now as long as I want to, I can wear what I like, do what I like. And I've a garden of my own."

" But you don't stop there," I said.

" Well," he said, " I wonder if you'd know what I meant if I said that a garden and sitting about is a bit too much for me for the present. I want to walk and walk in the open air, and see things, and stretch my legs a bit to get rid of twenty odd years of the bench.

29

I want to run up the top of hills and shout because—
well, because I feel as if I had a right to shout when
the sun is shining."

" I quite understand that," I said.

" And then," he went on, and his face showed the
joy he felt, " everything is so wonderful. Look at
that village we came through : those people there feel
the same as you and me. They've got to express themselves somehow, so they grow flowers right out into
the road, just as a gift to you and me. A sort of something comes to them that they must have flowers at the
front door. Whenever I see a good garden, full of
Pinks and Roses and Larkspur, I get a bed at that
cottage, if I can. I've slept all over the place, all over
England, you might say ; and cheap, too."

" That was a beautiful village, below there," I said.

He nodded wisely. " Seems as if they'd decorated
the street on purpose to make the cottages look
as if they grew like the flowers. All the porches
covered with Honeysuckle and Roses, and everlasting Peas, and flowers up against the windows.
I've a perfect craze for flowers—can't think where I
get it from."

" You are the real gardener," said I.

" I believe I am," he said. " And why I took to
tailoring beats me, now. My father was a butcher."

I pointed over my shoulder towards the village.
" Do you live in a place like that ? " I asked.

" Better than that," he answered proudly. " It
took me nearly two years to find the place my sister
and I had dreamed of. We wanted a cottage in a
county as much like a garden as possible. I found it—in
Devonshire ; my eye, it's a wonderful place, all orchards.
In the blossom time it looks like—well, as if it was
expecting somebody, it's so beautiful."

" I know," I said. " Sometimes the country dresses itself as if a lover were coming."

" Do you ever read Browning ? " he asked. " Because he answers a lot of questions for me."

" For me too."

" Well," he said, and reddened shyly as he said it ; " do you remember the poem that ends

' What if that friend happened to be God ? ' "

I understood perfectly. He was a man of soul, my tailor.

" I expect you are surprised to find I read a lot," he went on in his artless way. " But when I was a boy I was in a book shop, before my father lost all his money, and put me out to be a tailor. My mother was a lady's maid, and she encouraged me to read. There was a priest, Father Brown, who helped me too ; it was from him I first learned to love flowers."

" Then, as you are a Catholic, you know what to-day is," said I.

" The twenty-ninth of August. No, sir, I'm afraid I don't."

" It is dedicated to one of our patron Saints—there are two for gardeners—Saint Phocas, a Greek, and Saint Fiacre, an Irishman. To-day is the day of Saint Phocas."

The tailor crossed himself reverently.

" I'll tell you the story if you like." And, as he lay on his back, I told him the little legend of

SAINT PHOCAS : PATRON SAINT OF GARDENERS.

" At the end of the third century there lived a certain good man called Phocas, who had a little dwelling outside the gates of the city of Sinope, in Pontus. He had a small garden in which he grew flowers and

31

vegetables for the poor and for his own needs. Prayer, love of his labour, and care for the things he grew filled his life."

My tailor interrupted here to ask, apologetically, what manner of garden Saint Phocas would have.

" Neat beds," said I—for I had gone into the matter myself— " edged with box. The flowers and vegetables growing together. Violets, Leeks, Onions, with Crocuses, Narcissus, and Lilies. Then, in their season, Gladiolus, Hyacinths, Iris, Poppies, and plenty of Roses. Melons, also, and Gherkins, Peaches, Plums, Apples and Pomegranates, Olives, Almonds, Medlars, Cherries, and Pears, of which quite thirty kinds were known. In his house, on the window ledge, if he had one, he may have grown Violets and Lilies in window pots, for they did that in those days."

" Now, isn't that interesting ? " said the tailor. " My sister will care to know that. I shouldn't be a bit surprised to find her putting a statue of Saint Phocas over the door. She's all for figures."

" I'm afraid," said I, " there will be some trouble over that. There is a statue of him in Saint Mark's in Venice, a great old man with a fine beard, dressed like a gardener, and holding a spade in his hand. There's one of him, too, in the Cathedral at Palermo, but I have never seen them copied. Now I must tell you the rest of the story.

" There were days, you know, when Christians were hunted out and killed. One evening there came to the house of the Saint, two strangers. It was the habit of this good man to give of what he had to all travellers, food, rest, water to bathe their feet, and a kindly welcome. On this occasion the Saint performed his hospitable offices as usual—set the strangers at his board, prepared a meal for them, and led them afterwards to a

32

Beatrice Parsons

1. RHODODENDRONS

George S. Elgood, R.I.

2. EVENING PRIMROSE

Helen Allingham, R.W.S.

3. THE COTTAGE

w . Biscombe Gardner

4. THE WEALD OF KENT, SHOWING THE COUNTRY
LIKE A PATCHWORK QUILT

George S. Elgood, R.I.

5. THE CRIMSON RAMBLER

6. IN A SUMMER GARDEN

7. THE BLUEBELL WOOD

Agnes Locke

8. THE COTTAGE GARDEN

Sutton Palmer, R.I.

9. A SURREY COTTAGE

Helen Allingham, R.W.S.

10. THE STILE

Beatrice Parsons

11. A PERGOLA IN AN ENGLISH GARDEN

Beatrice Parsons

12. ENTRANCE TO THE GARDENS

Beatrice Parsons

13. A ROUND GARDEN

14. A WOOD AT WOTTON, THE HOME OF JOHN EVELYN

Sutton Palmer, R.I.

Beatrice Parsons

15. TULIPS IN THE GARDEN OF PEACE

George S. Elgood, R.I.

16. APPLE TREES

place where they might sleep. Before going to rest they told him their errand ; they were searching for a certain man of the name of Phocas, a Christian, and, having found him, they were to slay him. When they were asleep, the Saint, after offering up his prayers, went into his garden and dug a grave in the middle of the flower beds.

" The morning came, and the strangers prepared to depart, but the Saint, standing before them, told them he was the very man whom they sought. A horror seized them that they should have eaten with the man they had set out to kill, but Saint Phocas, leading them to the grave among the flowers, bid them do their work. They cut off his head, and buried him in his own garden, in the grave he had dug."

The little tailor was silent. I lit my pipe, and began to put my traps together.

Then he spoke. " I couldn't do that, you know. Those martyrs—by gum ! "

" Death," said I, " was life to them. Their life was only a preparation for death."

The tailor sat up. " My sister's like that," he said. " She's bought a tombstone—think of that. Said she'd like to have it by her. She's a one for a bargain, if you like ; saw this tombstone marked ' Cheap,' in a stonemason's yard down our way, and went in at once to ask the price. She'd price anything, my sister would. You've only got to mark a thing down ' Cheap ' and she's after the price in a minute."

" How did the tombstone come to be marked ' cheap ' ? " I asked, laughing with him.

" It was this way," said the tailor. Then he turned, in his inconsequent way to me. " I wonder," he said, " if, as you're so kind as to take an interest, you'd care to see our cottage. We'd be proud, my sister and

33

I, if you would come. If you are just walking about for pleasure, perhaps you'd come down as far as that one day and—and, well, sir, it's very humble, but we'd do our best."

" When shall you be there ? " I said. " Because I want to come very much."

" I'm going back ; I'm on my way now," he said ; " I always go back two or three times in the summer just to tell her the news. I tell her what's happened, and what flowers they grow where I've been. If you would really come, sir, perhaps you'd come in three weeks from now, if you have nothing better to do. I'd let her know."

" Then she could tell me the story of the tombstone herself ? " I said.

It ended at that. He wrote the address for me in my sketch-book, and took his leave of me in characteristic fashion.

" I hope I'm not taking a liberty," he said, as he jerked his knapsack into a comfortable place between his shoulders.

" There's nothing I should like better," said I.

" You'll like the garden," he said as an inducement.

And this was how I came to hear the story of the " Tailor's Sister's Tombstone."

VI

THE BLUEBELL WOOD AND THE CALM STONE DOG

MAN is an autobiographical animal, he speaks only from his thimbleful of human experience, and the I, I, I, of his talk drops out like an insistent drip of water. Even the knowledge we gain from books has to be grafted on to the knowledge we have of life before it bears fruit in our minds. Like patient clerks we are always adding up the columns of facts, fancies, and ideas, and arriving at the very tiny total at the end of the day.

In order to give themselves scope when they wish to soliloquise, many authors address their conversation to a cat, a grandfather clock, a dog, a picture on the wall, or what-not. Cats, I think, have the preference. I have often wondered what Crome, the painter, said to his cat when he pulled hairs out of her to make paint-brushes ; or what Doctor Johnson said to his cat Hodge, about Boswell. Having explained this much, I may easily be forgiven for repeating the conversation I had with a Stone Dog who sat on his haunches outside the door of a woodman's cottage.

The cottage stood on the edge of a wood, and was, as I shall point out, a remnant of departed glory, of which the dog was the most pertinent reminder.

A cottage on the borders of a wood is in itself one of the most valuable pictures for a romance. A wood-

35

cutter may be in league with goodness knows how many fairies, elves, and witches. It is a place where heroes meet heroines; where kings in disguise eat humble pie; where dukes, lost in hunting a white stag. meet enchanted princesses.

The wood, of which I speak, was once, years ago— about three hundred years—part of the park of Tanglewood Court, an extensive property, an old house, a great family possession.

Gone, like last winter's snow, were the family of Bois; gone the pack; gone the glories of the great family; gone the portraits, the armour, the very windows of Tanglewood Court, of which but a fine ruin remained. And the lane, a mere cart track, was all that was left of the fine sweep of drive to the house; and a tangled undergrowth under ancient trees all that stood for the grand avenue down which my Lord Bois had once ridden so madly. They call the lane Purgatory Lane, and they tell a story of wild doings and of a beautiful avenue, that cannot have its place here.

The great gates that once swung open to admit the carriage of Perpetua Bois (of the red hair, the full voluptuous figure, the smile Sir Peter Lely painted) were now two stone stumps at the feet of which two slots, green and worn, showed where the hinges had been. These fine gates once boasted, on the top of stone pillars, the greyhounds of Bois in stone. One of these dogs had been rescued from the undergrowth by the woodcutter, the other lies broken and bramble-covered in the wood. I wonder if they miss each other.

So you see I was addressing myself to a high-born Jacobean dog.

This dog, very calm and dignified, with a stone tail and a back worn smooth by wind and weather, sat

with his back to the cottage which had been built out
of the remains of the old stone lodge by a gentleman of
the name of Bellington, who was afterwards found
drowned in the lake. That lake held many secrets,
indeed, some said (the woodcutter's wife told me this)
it held Lady Perpetua's jewels. That did not con-
cern me, for it held for me the finer jewels of Water
Lilies that grew there in profusion, though I will not
deny that the idea of Lady Perpetua gave an added
touch of romance. How often had the clear water of
the lake reflected her satin-clad figure and the forms of
her little toy spaniels ?

It so happening, I sat by the Stone Dog, on a wooden
seat, to eat my lunch one day, and dropped into conversation with him, after a bite or two, in the most
natural way in the world.

There was the wood in front of us, blue-purple with
wild Hyacinths. There was the old cottage behind
clothed with rambling Creepers ; a carpet of smooth
rabbit-worn grass at our feet ; a profusion of Primroses, Wind Flowers, and budding trees before our
eyes. There was also the enchanting hum of wild bees
(like those wild bees Horace knew, that sought the
mountain of Matinus in Calabria, and there " laboriously
gathered the grateful thyme ") to soothe us in our
solitude.

I addressed him then, " Stone Dog," I said, " this
is a very beautiful wood. Nature, laughing at the
ghosts of the Bois family, steel-clad, periwigged, or
patched, has reclaimed her own."

The dog answered me never a word but kept his gaze
fixed in front of him as if he saw visions in the wood.

" This was a Park once," said I, " the pleasure-
ground of great folk, where they might sport in play-
ful dalliance "—I thought that sounded rather Jacobean.

But, as I looked at him, it seemed, as though he listened for the sound of wheels, and turned his sightless eyes to look for the figure of Lady Perpetua.

" She was very fair," I said, understanding him, knowing that he had seen many generations drive through the gates he sat to guard. " She would come down to the lodge-keeper's house to take her breakfast draught of small ale. Poor Lady Perpetua, she was a good house wife, and saw to the pickling of Nasturtium buds, and Lime Tree buds, and Elder roots ; and ordered the salting of the winter beef ; and looked to it that plenty of Parsnips were stored to eat with it. What sights you must have seen ! "

Even as I talked there emanated from the Stone Dog some atmosphere of the past, and we were once more in a fair English park, with its orangeries, and houses of exotic plants, and its maze, and leaden statues, and cut yew trees, and lordly peacocks. The great trees had been cut down, and the timber sold ; acres of land, once grazing ground for herds of deer, were ploughed ; here, in front of us, was the tangled wood, a corner of what was, once, a wild garden—a fancy of Lady Perpetua's, no doubt, who loved solitudes, and sentimental poetry :

"I could not love thee, dear, so much ;
Loved I not honour more."

Perhaps it was here she met young Hervey ; perhaps it was here Lord Bois found them, cutting initials on one of those very trees, G. H. and P. B. and two hearts with an arrow through them. Ah ! then the smile Sir Peter Lely painted faded to a quiver of the lips. Lord Bois looked at the trembling mouth and his glance flew to the initials on the tree. " So this is why, madam, I could hear him say, " you took to sylvan glades like a timid deer ; so this is why you coaxed me up to

38

London, leaving you alone—but, not unprotected." I could see his sneering bow to young Hervey—a bow that was a blow.

And all the while I was only seeing with the Stone Dog's eyes. There was just the rippling sea of wild Hyacinths, the pale gold of the Primroses, the innocent white of the wood Anemones—like fairies' washing— and the purple haze of bursting buds.

Once the Stone Dog had looked along an avenue and had seen a vista of Tanglewood Court, and smooth terraces, and bright beds of flowers, with Lords and Ladies walking up and down, taking the air, discussing fruit trees, and Dutch gardening, and glass hives for bees. Now, he saw nothing but the woods all brimming with Spring flowers : a garden made by Nature.

And then I thought I saw one Bluebell detach itself from its fellows and come wafting to us with a fairy's message, but it was a bright blue butterfly who sailed, rejoicing in the sun. Somehow the butterfly reminded me of the Lady Perpetua, soft and smiling, and fluttering in the sun : as if she had returned to her woods in that guise to hover near the tree, the trysting-place, on which the initials were cut.

I said as much to the Stone Dog, but received no answer.

" Stone Dog," I said, " England is a very wonderful place : every park, every field, every little wood is full of stories. I cannot pass a park gate without thinking of the men and women who have been through it. What a Garden of History the whole place is ! I'll warrant a Roman has kissed a Saxon girl in this very place, for there's a camp not far off—perhaps you have seen twinkling ghostly watch-fires gleaming in the night. Young Hervey's dead, but you never saw him die ; they fought in the garden on the smooth grass, and the story goes that he slipped, and Bois ran him through as he lay on the grass. What flowers grow over his head now ? And Perpetua is dead. They say she ran out and saw her lover dead, and bared her breast to her husband's sword. The grass was wet with her blood when you saw Lord Bois ride madly down the drive, through the gates, and out into the open country. The smile Sir Peter Lely painted is carved by the hand of Death. She was only a girl, after all. Who places flowers on her grave ? "

Meanwhile the sun shone on the Bluebells, and struck odd leaves of the trees, picking them out with a fanciful finger till they shone like green fires.

Then the idea came to me that this wood held the spirit of Lady Perpetua fast for ever. The Bluebells were the satin sheen of her dress (blue like the Lely portrait), the red-brown autumn leaves and the dead Bracken were her hair ; the Wind Flowers, like her body linen ; the Violets, her eyes ; the Primroses, her breath ; the Cowslips, her golden ornaments ; the Daisy petals like her pure white skin. A gentle breeze stirred all the flowers together, and—behold ! there she was, alive. The wood was yielding up her secret, as woods and flowers will do to those who love them.

So the Stone Dog and I had a bond of sympathy between us, the bond of old memories, and the wood united us with its store of romance and beauty : and he who loves wild flowers and woods, as well as walled gardens and trees clipped in images, may gather store of pictures for his mind.

So the afternoon passed in this pleasant manner, and I took opportunity to speak once more to the Stone Dog before the woodcutter's children came home from school to spoil our peace.

I said, " There is no man so poor but he can afford

40

to take pleasure in Bluebells, and, even if he live in a town, there are wild flowers for sale in the streets, and a bunch of Spring to be bought for a penny. And there is no man so rich that he can wall up the treasures of heaven, or build his walls so high but a Rose will peep over the edge. Poor and rich are free of their thoughts, and there are thoughts and enough to spare, in a hedgerow or a wood. Uncaged birds sing best, and wild flowers yield the purest scents. You and I are fellow dreamers, and this wood is our garden, and these birds our orchestra, and this grass our carpet ; and even when I am underneath the brown earth I love so well, you will sit here and listen for the sound of carriage wheels, and wonder if you will catch a glimpse of red hair and a satin dress through the long-silent avenue. There are mountains, Stone Dog, that still feel the pressure of the foot of Moses ; and hills under which Roman soldiers lie ; and there are woods growing where orchard gardens were ; and gardens planted where the wild boar once ravaged."

After I had said this came wild shouts, and the laughter of children, and a great clatter as the four children of the woodcutter came running from the village school.

As I left that place, and turned, before a bend of the road shut out the sight of the wood, I saw the sea of Bluebells, and the sky above, the Primroses and the Wind Flowers and last year's leaves all melt into one. The figure they made was the figure of Lady Perpetua standing there smiling. Then I heard the wheels of a carriage on the road, and I could have sworn I saw the Stone Dog turn his head.

41

VII

THE TAILOR'S SISTER'S TOMBSTONE

I WAS on the hill over against the village where my friend the tailor lived, and was preparing to descend into the valley to inquire the whereabouts of his cottage, when one of those sharp summer storms came on, the sky being darkened as if a hand had drawn a curtain across it, and the entire village lit by a vivid, unnatural light, like limelight in its intensity.

Turning about, as the first great drops fell, to look for shelter, I spied a rough shed by the wayside, shut in on three sides with gorse, wattle and mud, and roofed over with heather thatch. Into this I scuttled and found a comfortable seat on a sack placed on a pile of hurdles.

It was evidently a place used by a shepherd for a store-house of the implements of his craft. At the back of a shed was one of those houses on wheels shepherds use in the lambing season; besides this were hurdles, sacks, several rusty tins, and a very rusty oil-stove. All very primitive, and possessed of a nice earthy smell. It gave me a sudden desire to be a shepherd.

Looking down into the valley I saw men running for shelter, hastily pulling their coats over their shoulders as they ran. In a field on the far side of the valley they were carting Wheat, and I saw two men quickly unhitch the cart horses, and lead them away to some place hidden from me by trees.

42

THE TAILOR'S SISTER'S TOMBSTONE

The village was buried in orchards, and lay along the bank of a quickly running river that caught a glint of the weird light here and there between the trees like a path of shining silver. A squat church tower stuck up among the red roofs.

For a moment the scene shone in the fierce light, then the low growling thunder broke into a tremendous crash, and the light was gone in an instant. Then the rain blotted out everything.

The hiss of the rain on the dry heather thatch over my head was good enough company, and it was added to, soon, by the entrance of seven swallows that flew into my shelter and sat twittering on a beam just inside the opening. Then came an inky darkness, broken violently by a blare of lightning as if some hand had rent the dark curtain across in a rage. A great torn jagged edge of blue-white light streamed across the valley, showing everything in wet, glistening detail.

Only that morning I had been reading by the wayside an account of a storm in the Memoirs of Benvenuto Cellini. It came very pat for the day. It was at the time when Cellini rode from Paris carrying two precious vases on a mule of burden, lent him to go as far as Lyons, by the Bishop of Pavia. When they were a day's journey from Lyons, it being almost ten o'clock at night, such a terrific storm burst upon them that Cellini thought it was the day of judgment. The hailstones were the size of Lemons ; and the event caused him to sing psalms and wrap his clothes about his head. All the trees were broken down, all the cattle deprived of life, and a great many shepherds were killed.

I was still engaged in picturing this when the sky above me grew lighter, the rain fell less heavily, and, in a very short time, all that was left of the storm was

43

a distant sound as of a giant murmuring, a dark blot of rain cloud on the distant hills, and the ceaseless patter of dripping trees. The sun shone out and showed the village and landscape all fresh and shining. Then, as I looked, against the dark bank of distant clouds, a rainbow arched in glorious colours, one step of the arch on the hills tailing into mist, and one in the corn field below. The sight of the rainbow with its wonderful beauty, and its great message of hope thrilled me, as it always does. I do not care what the scientist tells me of its formation : he has not added one atom to my feeling, with all his knowledge. It remains for me the sign of God's compact with man.

" And God said, This is the token of the covenant which I make between me and you, and every living creature that is with you, for perpetual generations.

" I set my bow in a cloud, and it shall be for a token of a covenant between me and the earth.

" And it shall come to pass, when I bring a cloud over the earth, that the bow shall be seen in the cloud.

" And I will remember my covenant which is between me and you, and every living creature of all flesh ; and the waters shall no more become a flood to destroy all flesh.

" And the bow shall be in the cloud ; and I will look upon it, that I may remember the everlasting covenant between God and every living creature of all flesh that is upon the earth."

I learnt to love that when I was a child, and being still, in many ways, the same child, I look upon a rainbow and think of God remembering his covenant : and it makes me very happy.

Now as the storm was over, and I had no further excuse for stopping in my shelter, I took my knapsack again on to my shoulder and walked down, across two fields of grass, round the high hedges of two orchards, and came out into the road in the valley, about two hundred yards distant from the village church. It was about four of the afternoon.

I was about to turn towards the village to ask my best way to the tailor's cottage, when who should turn the bend of the road but the tailor himself with all the air of looking for some one.

I grasped him warmly by the hand, and he held mine in a good grip like the good fellow he was, saying, " I was looking about for you, sir, thinking you might have forgotten my direction " (as indeed, I had), " and knowing you would most likely go to the village to inquire, I was on my way there."

As we turned to walk down the road away from the church, the tailor informed me his sister was all agog to see me, but very nervous that I might think theirs too poor a place to put up with, and she had, at the last moment, implored him to take me to the inn instead.

The affection I had gained for the little man in my few hours' talk with him made me certain I should be happy in his company, and I laughed at his fears.

" Why, man," said I, " I have walked a good hundred miles to see you, do you think it likely I shall turn away at the last minute ? "

" There," cried the tailor, " I told her so. She's a small body, you'll understand, sir, and gets worried at times."

We turned a corner and I saw before me one of the prettiest cottages I have ever seen. A low, sloping roof of thatch, golden brown where it had been mended, rich brown and green in the older part. The body of the cottage was white, with a fine tree of Cluster Roses, the Seven Sisters, I think it is called, growing over the porch and on the walls. The garden was one mass of bloom, a wonderful garden—as artists say,

45

" juicy " with colour. Standard Roses, Sweet Williams, Hollyhocks, patches of Violas, Red Hot Pokers, Japanese Anemones, a hedge of Sweet Peas " all tip-toe for a flight " as Keats has it, clumps of Dahlias just coming out, with red pots on sticks to catch the earwigs ; an old Lavender hedge, grey-green. A rain butt painted green ; round a corner, three blue-coloured beehives ; and all about, such flowers—I could not mention half of them. Bushes of Phlox, for instance ; and great brown-eyed Sunflowers cracked across with wealth of seed ; and tall spikes of Larkspur like the summer skies : and Carnations couched in their grey grass or tied to sticks. A worn brick pathway leading through it all.

The tailor watched the effect on me anxiously.

I stood with one hand on the gate and drank in the beauty of it. Set, as the place was, in a bower of orchards, it looked like a jewelled nest, a place out of a fairy tale, everything complete. The diamond panes of the windows with neat muslin curtains behind them, with fine Geraniums in very red pots on the window-sill, were like friendly eyes beaming pleasantly at the passing world. To a tired traveller making his way upon that road, such a sight would bring delight to his eyes, and cause him, most certainly, to pause before the glad garden. If he were a romantic man he would take off his hat, as men do abroad to a wayside Calvary, in honour of the peace that dwelt over all.

Like a rich illuminated page the garden glowed among the trees—like a jewel of many colours it shone in its velvet nest.

The tailor could restrain himself no longer. He said, " As neat as anything you've seen, sir ? "

" Perfect," said I. " As much as a man could want."

He walked before me down the garden path and called, " Rose." through the open door.

THE TAILOR'S SISTER'S TOMBSTONE

In another minute I was shaking hands with the tailor's sister.

In appearance she was as spotlessly clean as her muslin curtains. She was a tiny woman of about forty-five, very quick in her movements, with a little round red face and very bright blue eyes. She wore, in my honour, a black silk dress, and a black silk apron and a large cornelian brooch at her neck.

" Pray step inside, sir," she said throwing open the door of the parlour.

When I was seated at tea with these people I kept wondering where they had learnt the refinement and taste everywhere exhibited. For one thing the few family possessions were good, and there was no tawdry rubbish. A grandfather clock, its case shining with polishing, ticked comfortably in one corner of the room. An old-fashioned sofa filled the window space. We sat upon Windsor chairs with our feet on a rag carpet. Most of the household gods were over or upon the mantelpiece, most prominent among which was a really fine landscape, hung in the centre. I inquired whose work this might be.

One had only to look in the direction of any object to get its history from the tailor.

" I bought that, sir," he said, when I was looking at the picture, " of a man near Norwich. It cost me half a crown."

" Three shillings," said the sister. Then to me, " He takes a sixpence off, now and again, sir, because he's jealous of my bargains ; aren't you, Tom ? "

Tom smiled at her and winked at me. " She will have her bit of fun," he said.

" But it's a fine picture," said I.

" Proud to have you say so," he answered ; " I like it, and the man didn't seem to care about it. He was

47

going to the Colonies and parting with a lot of odds and ends. I bought the brass candlesticks off him at the same time—a shilling."

I could see why the little man liked the picture, for the same reason I liked it myself. It was of the Norwich School, a broad open landscape painted with care and finish of detail, and with much of the charming falsity of light common among certain pictures of that time. On the left was a cottage whose garden gave on to the road, a cottage almost buried under two great trees. The road wound past, out of the shadows of the trees, and vanished over a hill. The middle distance showed a great expanse of country dotted with trees with the continuation of the road running through the vale until it was lost in a wood. A sky of banked up clouds hung over all. Right across the middle of the picture was a wonderfully painted gleam of sunlight, flicking trees, meadows, and the road into bright colours ; the rest of the picture being subdued to give this effect. Up the road, coming towards the cottage, was a small man in a three-cornered hat, knee breeches, and long skirted coat. This figure dated the picture a little earlier than I had at first thought it.

" That's me," said the tailor, pointing to the figure. " That's what Rose said as soon as I brought it home, ' Why that's you, Tom.' "

" I did, sir, that's just what I said. ' Why Tom, that's you,' I said."

" And so it is," said the tailor.

Half a crown ! Few of us are rich enough in taste to have bought it.

After tea I begged leave to see the garden. " And, Miss Rose," I said, " to hear about the tombstone, please."

She put her small fat hands to her face and laughed

and laughed. " He's been and told you that, sir ?
Well, I never did ! "

We went out of the back door and into a second
flower garden rivalling the one in front for a display
of colour. There, sure enough, stood the tombstone,
grey and upright, planted in a bed of flowers. They
seemed to hurl themselves at the grim object, wave
upon wave of coloured joy washing the feet of the
emblem of Death.

" There she is," said the tailor's sister proudly.

" Please tell me about it," said I, wondering at her
cheerfulness.

" You see, sir," she began, " before Tom and I came
into our fortune, and got rich——"

Multi-millionaires, I thought, could you but hear
that ! But they were rich—as rich as any one could
be. The flowers in the garden were worth a kingdom.

" —We used to wonder what we'd do if we ever had
a bit of money. Of course, we never dreamed of anything like this." Her eyes wandered proudly over her
possessions.

" Yes," said the tailor, joining in. " Our best dreams
never came near this. I'd seen such places, but never
thought to live in one, much less own one."

" Well, you see, sir," said his sister taking up the
thread of her story, " there was one thing I'd always
set my mind on—a nice place to lie in when I was dead.
I had a horror of cemeteries, great ugly places, as you
might say, with the tombstones sticking up like almonds
in a tipsy cake pudding, and a lot of dirty children
playing about. I lived for ten years in London, in a
room that overlooked one, a most dingy place I called
it. I couldn't bear to think I'd be popped in with a
crowd, anyhow. Now, a churchyard in the country—
that's quite different."

49

" I'd a great fancy for a spot I knew in Kent," said the tailor. " Dark Yew trees all round one side, and Daisies over everything, and a seat near by for people to rest on, coming early to church."

" Go on, Tom," said his sister lovingly. " Ar'n't you satisfied with what you've got ? "

He turned to me after putting his arm through his sister's. " We've got our piece of ground," he said cheerfully. " I'm going to be planted next to her, on the left of the church door—well, it's as good a place as you'd find anywhere, and people coming out of church will notice us easily. I'd like to be thought of, after I'm gone."

Death held no terrors for these people, it seemed, they talked so happily of it, made such delightful plans to welcome it ; robbed it of all its gloom and horror, its false trappings, its dingy grandeur.

There was a flaunting Red Admiral sunning its wings on the tombstone.

" I never thought," said the sister, " I should find just what I wanted by accident. Isn't it lovely ? "

It certainly had a beauty of its own. It was a copy of an early eighteenth century tombstone, the top in three arches, the centre arch large, and round, ending in carved scroll work. In the centre of the arch a cherub was carved, very fat and smiling, with wings on either side of his head. Then, in good deep-cut lettering, were the words :

SACRED TO THE MEMORY

OF

ROSE BRANDLE

Both these curious people looked at me as I read the lettering. Arm in arm they looked nice, cheerful, loving friends, a good deal like one another in the face, very gay and homely, and with a certain sparkling brightness, like the flowers they loved. To see them standing there proudly, smiling at the grey tombstone, smiling at me, under the sun, in the garden so full of life and of growing healthy things, gave me a sensation that Death was present in friendly guise, a constant welcome companion to my new friends, and a pleasant image even to myself.

" Second-hand," said the tailor's sister, " all except the name, and he put that in for me at a penny the letter : that came to elevenpence, so I gave him a shilling to make an even sum."

" A guinea, as it stands," said the tailor.

" You like it, sir ? " asked his sister anxiously.

" On the contrary," said I, " I admire it enormously."

" As soon as I saw it," she said, " I fell in love with it. It was standing at the back of the yard among a heap of stones. The sun was shining on it, and I said to myself, ' If that's cheap, it's as good as mine.' The man had cut it out years ago as an advertisement to put in the front of the yard, and it had a bit of paper pasted on it with his terms and what not—Funerals in the best style. Distance no object—and that sort of thing. I asked the price of it and he told me ' One pound.' ' Cheap,' I said, and he told me how 'twas so, since people nowadays like broken urns and pillars or something plainer, and had given up cherubs, and death-heads and suchlike. So I put down the money, and he popped it on a waggon that was coming back this way with a small load of Hay, and Tom put it up for me in the garden. Now I can die happy, sir."

I asked her if she had no feelings about Death, and if the idea of leaving her garden and her cottage was not strange to her.

She replied, in the simplest way possible, being a

51

cheerful religious woman without a particle of sham in her nature, that when God called her she was ready and glad to go, and as for the garden she would only go to another one—far more beautiful.

Her faith, I found afterwards, was of a sweet simple kind, and had been with her as a child, and remained with her as a woman, untouched by the least doubt. She heard Mass every morning of her life in the little church half a mile away, and spoke in loving and familiar tones of her favourite saints as being friends of hers, though in a higher station of life. Included in her ideas of heaven was a very distinct belief that there would be many beautiful flowers and birds, and the pleasure with which she looked forward to seeing them —in a humble way, as if she might be one of a crowd in a Public Garden—gave her a quiet dignity and charm, the equal of which I have seldom met. Her brother, who was always marvelling at her, had, also, some of her dignity, but a wider, freer view of things, and the natural gaiety of a bird.

The next morning, as soon as I woke in the fresh clean bedroom they had made ready for me, I sprang from my bed and went to look out of the window. The dew was sparkling on the flowers, and their scent came up sweet and strong ; a tubful of Mignonette, at which the bees were busy, was especially fragrant. As I looked, the tailor's sister came into the garden, in a neat lavender-coloured print dress ; she carried a missal in one hand, and a rosary swung in the other. She stood opposite to her tombstone for a minute, her lips moving softly, and then, after turning her pleasant face towards the wealth of flowers about her, she bowed deeply, as if saluting the morning. A little time later I heard the gate of the front garden swing and shut, and I knew she had gone to hear Mass.

THE TAILOR'S SISTER'S TOMBSTONE

The garden was left alone, busy in its quiet way ; growing, dying, perpetuating its kind. The bees were industriously singing as they worked ; lordly butter-flies danced rigadoons and ravanes over the flowers ; a thrush, after a long hearty tug at a fat worm, swallowed it, and then, perching on the tombstone, poured out its joy in full clear notes. And Death was cheated of his sting.

VIII

THE COTTAGE GARDEN

FOR the same reason that your town man keeps a pot
of Geraniums on his window-sill, and a caged bird in
his house, your countryman plants bright-coloured
flowers by his door, and regales his children with news
of the first cuckoo. They pull as much of Heaven down
as will accommodate itself to their plot of earth.

Any man standing in the centre of however small a
space of his personal ownership—a piece of drugget
in a garret, a patch of garden—makes it the hub of the
universe round which the stars spin, on which his world
revolves. Within a hand-stretch of him lie all he is,
his intimate possessions, his scraps of comfort scratched
out of the hard earth : books, pictures, photographs
showing the faces of his small world of friends and his
tiny travels—how little difference there is between a
walk through Piccadilly and a journey across Asia :
your great traveller has little more to say than the
man who has found Heaven in a penny bunch of Violets,
or heard the stars whisper over St. James's Park—
within his reach are the things he has paid the price of
life for, and they are the cloak with which he covers his
nakedness of soul against the all-seeing eye he calls his
Destiny.

With all this, commenced perhaps in cowardice—
for the earth's brown crust is too like a grave, the garret
floor too like a shell of wood—your man, town or

54

country, grown to know love of little things, nurses a seedling as if it were his conscience, patches his drugget as if it were a verse he'd like to polish. Out of the vast dreary waste of faces who pass by unheeding, and the unseeing world that does not care whether he lives or dies, he makes his small hoard of treasures, as a child hides marbles, thinking them precious stones— as, indeed, they are to those who have eyes to see— and, be they books, or pictures, pots of plants, or curious conceits in china, they all answer for flowers, for the bright-coloured spots of comfort in a life of doubt.

No man thinks this out carefully, and sets about to plan his garden in this spirit : he feels a need, and meets it as he can. In this manner we are all cottage gardeners.

In days gone by—days of serfdom, oppression, battle, slavery, poverty—the countryman passed his day waiting for the next blow, living between pestilences, and praying in the dark for small sparks of comfort. The monks kept the land sweet by growing herbs in sheltered places ; the countryman looked dully at Periwinkles and Roses and Columbines, thought them pretty, and passed by. Even the meanest flower, Shepherd's-eye or Celandine, was too high for him to reach. (The poet who keeps Jove's Thunder on his mantelpiece would understand that.) Roses were common enough even in the dark ages ; the English hedgerow threw out its fingers of Wild Rose and scented the air—but where was the man with a nose for fragrance when a mailed hand was on his shoulder. Those Roses on the Field of Tewkesbury—think of them stained with blood and flowering over rotting corpses.

> " I sometimes think that never blows so red
> The Rose as where some buried Cæsar bled ;
> That every Hyacinth the Garden wears
> Dropt in its lap from some once lovely Head

And this delightful Herb whose tender Green
Fledges the River's Lip on which we lean.
Ah, lean upon it lightly ! for who knows
From what once lovely Lip it springs unseen."

Little did the dull ploughman think of Roses in the
hedge, or Violets in the bank, he'd little care except
for a dish of Pulse.   Yet, all the time, curious men were
studying botany, dredging the earth for secrets, as the
astronomer swept the sky.   The Arviells, Gilbert and
Hernicus, were, one in Europe, the other in Asia, collecting good plants and herbs to replenish the Jardins de
Santé the monks kept—that in the thirteenth century,
too, with war clouds everywhere, and steel-clad knights
wooing maidens in castles by the secondhand means of
luting troubadours.

The Arts of Rome were dead, buried, and cut up by
the plough.   (How many ploughmen, such as Chaucer
knew, turned long brown furrows over Roman vineyards, and black crows, following, pecked at bright
coins, brought by the plough to light.)

All at once, it must have seemed, the culture of flowers,
was in the air : Carnations became the rage ;   then
men spent heaven knows what on a Tulip bulb ;   built
orangeries ;   sent Emissaries abroad to cull flowers in
the East.   The great men's gardeners, great men themselves, kept flowers in the plot of ground about their
cottages ;   gave out a seed or so here and there ;   talked
garden gossip at the village ale-house.   (Tradescant
steals Apricots from Morocco into England.   A Carew
imports Oranges.   The Cherry orchards at Sittingbourne
are planted by one of Henry the Eighth's gardeners.
Peiresc brings all manner of flowers to bloom under
our grey skies : great numbers of Jessamines, the clay-
coloured Jessamine from China ; the crimson American
kind ; the Violet-coloured Persian.)

56

THE COTTAGE GARDEN

The grass piece by the cottage door begins to find itself cut into beds; uncared for flowers, wild Gillyflowers, Thyme, Violets and the like, give colour to the cottage garden that has only just become a garden. With that comes competition : one man outdoes another, begs plants and seeds of all his friends ; buds a Rose on to a Briar standard, and boasts the scent of his new Clove Pinks. And so it grew that times were not so strenuous : Queen Victoria comes to the throne, and with prosperity come the pretty frillings of life, and cottage gardens ape their masters' Rose walks, and collections of this and that. To-day Africa and Asia nod together in a sunny cottage border, and Lettuces from the Island of Cos show their green faces next to Sir Walter Raleigh's great gift to the poor man, the Potato. Poplars from Lombardy grow beside the garden gate ; the Currant bush from Zante drips its jewel-like fruit tassels under a Cherry tree given to us, indirectly, by Lucullus, lost by us in our slumbering Saxon times, and here again, with Henry the Eighth's gardener, from Flanders. In some quite humble gardens the Cretan Quince and Persian Peach grow ; so that history, poetry, and romance peer over Giles's rustic hedge ; and the wind blows scents of all the world through the small latticed window.

Ploughman Giles, sitting by his cottage door, smoking an American weed in his pipe while his wife shells the Peas of ancient Rome into a basin, does not realise that his little garden, gay with Indian Pinks and African Geraniums, and all its small crowd of joyous-coloured flowers, is an open book of the history of his native land spread at his feet. Here's the conquest of America, and the discovery of the Cape, and all the gold of Greece for his bees to play with. Here's his child making a chain of Chaucer's Daisies ; and there's a Chinese

57

mandarin nodding at him from the Chrysanthemums ; and there's a ghost in his cabbage patch of Sir Anthony Ashley of Wimbourne St. Giles in Dorsetshire.

Ploughman Giles is a fortunate man, and we, too, bless his enterprise and his love of striking colours and good perfumes when we lean over the gate of his cottage garden to give him good-day.

I showed him once a photograph of a picture by Holbein—the Merchant of the Steel Yard—and pointed out the vase of flowers on the table and the very same flowers growing side by side in his garden, Carnations, the old single kind, and single Gilly-flower. He looked at the picture with his glasses cocked at the proper angle on his nose—he's an oldish man and short-sighted —and said in his husky voice, " Well, zur, I be surprised to zee un."   And he called out his wife to look— which didn't please her much as she was cooking—but, when she saw the flowers, " In that there queer gentleman's room, and as true as life, so they do be," she became enthusiastic, wiped her hands many times on her apron, and looked from the picture to the actual flowers growing in her garden with a kind of awe and wonder. It was of far more interest to them to know that they were hand in glove with the history of their own country than it would have been to learn that chemists made a wonderful drug called digitalis out of the Foxgloves by the fence. I gave them the photograph and it hangs in a proud position next to a stuffed and bloated perch in a glass-case ; and, what is more, they have an added sense of dignity from the dim, far away time the picture represents to them.

" He might a plucked they flowers in this very garden," she says ; and indeed, he might if he had happened that way.   But the older flowers, though they don't realise it, are the people themselves.   Ploughman Giles and his

58

wife, have been on the very spot far, far longer than the Pinks and Gilly-flowers, blooming into ripe age, rearing countless families back and back and back, until one can almost see a Giles sacrificing to Thor and Odin at the stone on the hill behind the cottage. The Norman Church throws its shadow over the graves of countless Gileses, and over the graves, pleasant-eyed English Daisies shine on the grass.

After all, when we see a cottage standing in its glowing garden, with a neat hedge cutting it off from its fellows; with children playing eternal games with dolls (Mr. Mould's children following the ledger to its long home in the safe—shall I ever forget that?), we see the whole world, cares, joys, birth, death and marriage; the wealth of nations scattered carelessly in flowers, spoils from every continent, surrounded by a hedge, its own birds to sing, its hundred forms of life, feeding, breeding, dying round the cottage door; and, at night, its little patch of stars overhead.

It was a fanciful child, perhaps, but children are full of quaint ideas, who caught the moon in a bright tin spoon, and put it in a bottle, and drew the cork at night to let the moon out to sail in the sky. The child found the tin spoon, dropped by a passing tinware pedlar, in the road, waited till night came, with his head full of a fairy story he had heard, and when it was dark, except for the moon, he stepped into the garden, held the bowl of the spoon to catch the moon's reflection, and when she showed her yellow face distorted in the bright spoon, he poured the reflection, very solemnly, into a bottle and corked it fast and tight. Then, with a whispered fairy spell, some nurse's gibberish, he took the precious bottle and hid it in a cupboard along with other mysterious tokens. That's a symbol of all our lives, bottling up moons and letting them out at nights. Isn't a garden just such a dream-treat to some of us ? There are golden Marigolds for the sun we live by, and silver Daisies for the stars, and blue Forget-me-nots for summer skies. Heaven at our feet, and angels singing from birds' throats among the trees.

Sometimes we see one cottage garden, next to a Paradise of colour, flaunting Geraniums, and all the summer garland, and in it a poor tree or so, a few ill-kept weedy flowers, overgrown Stocks, a patch of drunken-looking Poppies, a grass-grown waste of choked Pinks : the whole place with a sullen air. What is the matter with the people living there ? A decent word will beg a plant or two, seeds and cuttings can be had for the asking. Is it a poor or a proud spirit who refuses to join the other displays of colour ? Knock at the door, and your answer comes quick-footed ; it is the poor spirit answers you. Of course, there are men who can coax blood out of a stone, and find big strawberries in the bottom of the basket ; and others who cannot grow anything, try as they may. It is common enough to hear this or that will not grow for so-and-so, or that man makes such a plant flourish where mine all die. There's something between man and his flowers, some sympathy, that makes a Rose bloom its best for one, and Carnations wither under his touch, or Asters show their magic purples for one, and give a weak display for another. No one knows what speaks in the man to the Roses that bloom for him, or what distaste Carnations feel for all his ministrations, but the fact remains—any gardener will tell you that. So with your man of greenhouses, so with your humble cottage gardener, and, looking along a village street, the first glance will show you not who loves the flowers but whom flowers love.

THE COTTAGE GARDEN

This, of course, is not the reason of the weedy garden of the poor spirit, the reason for that is obvious : the poor spirit never rejoices, and to grow and care for flowers is a great way of rejoicing. There's many a man sows poems in the spring who never wrote a line of verse : his flowers are his contribution to the world's voice ; united in expressions of joy, the writer, the painter, the singer, the flower-grower are all part of one great poem.

The average person who passes a cottage garden is more moved by the senses than the imagination ; he or she drinks deep draughts of perfume, takes long comfort to the eyes from the fragrant and coloured rood of land. They do not cast this way and that for curious imaginings ; it might add to their pleasure if they did so. There are men who find the whole of Heaven in a grain of mustard seed ; and there are those who, in all the pomp and circumstance of a hedge of Roses, find but a passing pleasure to the eye.

We, who take our pleasure in the Garden of England, who feast our eyes on such rich schemes of colours she affords, have reason to be more than grateful to those who encourage the cottage gardener in his work. It is from the vicarage, rectory, or parsonage gardens that most encouragement springs ; it is the country clergyman and his wife who, in a large measure, are responsible for the good cottage gardening we see nearly everywhere. These, and the numberless societies, combine to keep up the interest in gardening and bee-keeping, to which we owe one of our chiefest English pleasures. The good garden is the purple and fine linen of the poor man's life ; poets, philosophers, and kings have praised and sung the simple flowers that he grows. Wordsworth for instance, sings of a flower one finds in nearly every cottage garden :

61

LOVE-LIES-BLEEDING.

You call it " Love-lies-Bleeding "—so you may,
Though the red Flower, not prostrate, only droops
As we have seen it here from day to day,
From month to month, life passing not away :
A flower how rich in sadness !   Even thus stoops,
(Sentient by Grecian sculpture's marvellous power)
Thus leans, with hanging brow and body bent
Earthward in uncomplaining languishment,
The dying Gladiator.   So, sad Flower !
('Tis Fancy guides me, willing to be led
Though by a slender thread)
So drooped Adonis bathed in sanguine dew
Of his death-wound, when he from innocent air
The gentlest breath of resignation drew ;
While Venus in a passion of despair
Rent, weeping over him, her golden hair
Spangled with drops of that celestial shower.
She suffered, as Immortals sometimes do ;
But pangs more lasting far that Lover knew
Who first, weighed down by scorn, in some lone bower
Did press this semblance of unpitied smart
Into the service of his constant heart,
His own dejection, downcast Flower ! could share
With thine, and gave the mournful name
  Which thou wilt ever bear.

Then again, Mrs. Browning, who loved Nature and
England, and spoke her love in such delicate fancies,
writes of flowers in " Our Gardened England," in a poem
called,

A FLOWER IN A LETTER.

Red Roses, used to praises long,
Contented with the poet's song,
 The nightingale's being over ;
And Lilies white, prepared to touch
The whitest thought, nor soil it much,
 Of dreamer turned to lover.

THE COTTAGE GARDEN

Deep Violets you liken to
The kindest eyes that look on you,
   Without a thought disloyal !
And Cactuses a queen might don
If weary of her golden crown,
   And still appear as royal !

Pansies for ladies all ! I wis
That none who wear such brooches miss
   A jewel in the mirror :
And Tulips, children love to stretch
Their fingers down, to feel in each
   Its beauty's secret nearer.

Love's language may be talked with these !
To work out choicest sentences,
   No blossoms can be neater—
And, such being used in Eastern bowers,
Young maids may wonder if the flowers
   Or meanings be the sweeter.

IX

A FEAST OF WILD STRAWBERRIES

There's many a child has crowned her head with
Buttercups—no bad substitute for gold—mirrored her
face in a pool, and dreamed she was a Queen. There's
many a boy has lain for hours in the Wild Thyme on a
cliff top and sent dream-fleets to Spain. The touch of
imagination is all that is required to make the world
seem real, and not until that wand is used is the world
real. Only those moments when we hear the stars,
peer in through Heaven's gates, or rub shoulders with
a poet's vision, are real and substantial; the rest is
only dreamland, vague, unsatisfactory. Huddled rows
of dingy houses, smoke, grime, roar of traffic, scramble
for the pence that make the difference, these things are
not abiding thoughts—" Here there is no abiding city "
—but those great moments when we grow as the flowers
grow, sing as the birds sing, and feel at ease with the
furthest stars, those are the moments we live in and
remember. Our great garden may hold our thoughts
if we wish. When we own England with our eyes, when
all the fields and woods, the mountain streams, the
pools and rills, rivers and ponds, are ours; when
we are on our own ground with Ling and Broom,
Heather, Heath and Furze for our carpet; when
Harebells ring our matin's bell and Speedwell close
the day for us; when the Water-lily is our cup,
broad leaves of Dock our platter, and King-cups

A FEAST OF WILD STRAWBERRIES

our array—how vast!—of gold plate, then are we kings indeed.

I'll give you joy of all your hot-house fruit, if you'll leave me to my Wild Strawberries. I'll wish you pleasure of Signor What's-his-name, the violin player, if you'll but listen to my choir of thrushes. What do you care to eat? Here's nothing over substantial, I'll admit; but there's good wine in the brook, and food for a day in the fields and hedges. Nuts, Blackberries, Wortle-berries, Wild Raspberries, Mushrooms, Crabs and Sloes, and Samphire for preserving; Elderberries to make into a cordial; and Wild Strawberries, that's my chiefest dish at this season—food for princesses.

Come to the cliffs with your leaf of Wild Straw-berries, and I can show you blue Flax, and Sea Pinks, yellow Sea-Cabbage, and Sea Convolvulus, and Golden Samphire; you shall have Sandwort, and Viper's Bugloss, and Ploughman's Spikenard, and Horned Poppies, and Thyme, in plenty. We will choose a fanciful flower for the table, the yellow Elecampane that gave a cosmetic to Helen of Troy. And the mention of her who set Olympus and Earth in a blaze of discord makes me remember how Hermes, of the golden wand, gave to Odysseus the plant he had plucked from the ground, black at the root, and with a flower like to milk—" Moly the Gods call it, but it is hard for mortal men to dig; howbeit with the Gods all things are possible."

Any manner of imaginings may come to those who make a feast of Wild Strawberries. We may follow our Classic idea and discuss the Hydromel, or cider of the Greeks; the syrup of squills they drank to aid their digestion, or the absinthe they took to promote appetite. We might even try to make one of their sweet wines of Rose leaves and honey, such a thing would go well

65

with our Wild Strawberries. These things might all come out of our country garden and give us a ghostly Greek flavour for our pains.   There were Wild Strawberries, I think, on Mount Ida where Paris was shepherd, whence they fetched him when Discord threw the Golden Apple.

It is almost impossible to reach out a hand and pick a flower without plucking a lege.. ' with it.

I had taken, I thought, England for my garden, and Wild Strawberries for my dish, but I find that I have taken the world for my flower patch, and am sitting to eat with ancient Greeks.   Let me but pick the Pansy by my hand and I find that Spenser plucked its fellow years ago :

"Strew me the ground with Daffe-down-dillies,
    And Cowslips, and King-cups, and loved Lilies,
        The pretty Paunce (that is my wild Pansy)
        The Chevisaunce
    Shall watch with the fayre Fleur de Luce."

And you may call it Phœbus'-paramour, or Herb-Trinity, or Three Faces-under-a-Hood.

To our forefathers the fields, lanes, and gardens were a newspaper far more valuable than the modern sheet in which we read news of no importance day by day To them the blossoming of the Sloe meant the time for sowing barley ; the bursting of Alder buds that eels had left their winter holes and might be caught. The Wood Sorrel and the cuckoo came together ; when Wild Wallflower is out bees are on the wing, and linnets have learnt their spring songs. Water Plantain is supposed to cure a mad dog, and is a remedy against the poison of a rattlesnake ; ointment of Cowslips removes sunburn and freckles ; the Self-heal is good against cuts and so is called also, Carpenter's Herb, Hook-heal, and Sicklewort. Yellow Water-lilies will drive cockroaches and crickets from a house. Most charming intelligence of all deals with the Wild Canterbury Bell, in which the little wild bees go to sleep, loving their silky comfort. These are but a few paragraphs from our news-sheet, but they serve to show how pleasant a paper it is to know—and it costs nothing but a pair of loving and careful eyes.

If we choose to be more fanciful—and who is not, in a wild garden with a dish of Wild Strawberries ?—we shall find ourselves filling Acorn cups with dew to drink to the fairies, and wondering how the thigh of a honey-bee might taste. Herrick is the poet for such flights of thought. His songs—" To Daisies, not to shut so soon." " To Primroses filled with Morning Dew," and, for this instance, to

THE BAG OF THE BEE

About the sweet bag of a bee
  Two Cupids fell at odds ;
And whose the pretty prize should be
  They vowed to ask the Gods.

Which Venus hearing, thither came
  And for their boldness stripped them ;
And taking thence from each his flame
  With rods of Myrtle whipped them.

Which done, to still their wanton cries,
  When quiet grown she's seen them,
She kissed and wiped their dove-like eyes,
  And gave the bag between them.

We can do no better than give thanks for all our garden, our house, and our well-being in the words of the same poet. For we need to thank, somehow, for all the joys Nature gives us. Though, in

67

this poem, he names no flowers, yet his poems are
full of them :

" —That I, poor I,
May think, thereby,
I live and die
'Mongst Roses."

Every man who is a gardener at heart, whether he be
in love with the flowers of the open fields, the garden
of the highways and the woods, or with his protected
patch of ground, will care to know this song of Herrick's
if he has not already found it for himself :

A THANKSGIVING TO GOD FOR HIS HOUSE

Lord, thou hast given me a cell,
Wherein to dwell ;
A little house, whose humble roof
Is waterproof ;
Under the spars of which I lie
Both soft and dry ;
Where thou, my chamber for to ward,
Hast set a guard
Of harmless thoughts, to watch and keep
Me, while I sleep.
Low is my porch, as is my fate ;
Both void of state ;
And yet the threshold of my door
Is worn by th' poor,
Who thither come, and freely get
Good words or meat.
Like as my parlour, so my hall
And kitchen's small ;
A little buttery, and therein
A little bin,
Which keeps my little loaf of bread
Unchipt, unflead ;
Some brittle sticks of Thorn or Briar
Make me a fire

A FEAST OF WILD STRAWBERRIES

Close by whose living coal I sit,
   And glow like it.
Lord, I confess too, when I dine,
   The Pulse is thine.
And all those other bits that be
   There placed by Thee ;
The Worts, the Purslain, and the mess
   Of Watercress,
Which of thy kindness thou hast sent;
   And my content
Makes those, and my beloved Beet,
   To be more sweet.
'Tis thou that crown'st my glittering hearth,
   With guiltless mirth,
And giv'st me wassail bowls to drink,
   Spiced to the brink.
Lord, 'tis thy plenty-dropping hand
   That soils my land,
And giv'st me, for my bushel sown,
   Twice ten for one ;
Thou mak'st my teeming hen to lay
   Her egg each day ;
Besides, my healthful ewes to bear
   Me twins each year ;
The while the conduits of my kine
   Run cream, for wine ;
All these, and better, thou dost send
   Me, to this end—
That I should render, for my part,
   A thankful heart ;
Which, fired with incense, I resign,
   As wholly thine ;
—But the acceptance, that must be,
   My Christ, by Thee.

X

THE PRAISES OF A COUNTRY LIFE

TRANSLATED FROM HORACE

BY CHRISTOPHER SMART

HAPPY the man, who, remote from business, after the manner of the ancient race of mortals, cultivates his paternal lands with his own oxen, disengaged from every kind of usury ; his is neither alarmed with the horrible trumpet, as a soldier, nor dreads he the angry sea ; he shuns both the bar, and the proud portals of men in power.

Wherefore, he either weds the lofty Poplars to the mature branches of the Vine ; or lopping off the useless boughs with his pruning-knife, he engrafts more fruitful ones ; or takes a prospect of the herds of his lowing cattle, wandering about in a lonely vale ; or stores his honey, pressed from the combs, in clean vessels ; or shears his tender sheep.

Or, when Autumn has lifted up in the field his head adorned with mellow fruits, how glad is he while he gathers Pears grafted by himself, and the Grape that vies with the purple, with which he may recompense thee, O Priapus, and thee, father Sylvanus, the guardian of his boundaries !

Sometimes he delights to lie under an aged Holm, sometimes on the matted grass : meanwhile the waters glide down from steep clefts ; the birds warble in the woods ; and the fountains murmur with their purling streams, which invites gentle slumbers.

But when the wintry season of the tempestuous air prepares rains and snows, he either drives the fierce boars, with dogs on every side, into the intercepting toils ; or spreads his thin nets with the smooth pole, as a snare for the voracious thrushes ; or catches in his gin the timorous hare, or that stranger, the crane, pleasing rewards for his labour.

Amongst such joys as these, who does not forget those mischievous anxieties, which are the property of love ? But if a chaste wife, assisting on her part in the management of the house and beloved children, (such as is the Sabine, or the sunburnt spouse of the industrious Apulian) piles up the sacred hearth with old wood, just at the approach of her weary husband, and shutting up the fruitful cattle in the woven hurdles milks dry their distended udders ; and drawing this year's wine out of a well-seasoned cask, prepares the unbought collation ; not the Lucrine oysters could delight me more, nor the turbot, nor the scar, should the tempestuous Winter drive any from the Eastern floods to this sea : not the turkey, nor the Asiatic wild fowl, can come into my stomach more agreeable than the Olive, gathered from the richest branches of the trees, or the Sorrel that loves the meadows, or Mallows salubrious for a sickly body, or a lamb slain at the feast of the god Terminus, or a kid just rescued from a wolf.

Amidst these dainties, how it pleases one to see the well-fed sheep hastening home ? To see the weary oxen, with drooping neck, dragging the inverted plough-share ! and numerous slaves, the test of a rich family ranged about the smiling household gods !

71

PART II
GARDENS AND HISTORY

I

THE ROMAN GARDEN IN ENGLAND

It would appear, judging from the specimens one sees, that the building of garden apartments, or summer-houses, is a lost art. But then leisure, as an art, has also been lost ; and no man unless he understand leisure can possibly build an apartment to be entirely devoted to it.

Imagine the man of the day who could write of his summer-house as the younger Pliny wrote : " At the end of the terrace, adjoining to the gallery, is a little garden-apartment, which I own is my delight. In truth it is my mistress : 1 built it." The younger Pliny, of to-day, is scouring the countryside in a motor-car, his eyes half-blinded by dust, his nose offended by the stink of petrol ; his thoughts, like his toys, purely mechanical.

There are still a few quiet people, and some scholars, whom the Socialist in his eager desire to benefit man-kind at reckless speed, and at ruthless expense of humanity, would like to blot out, who can enjoy their gardens with that curious remoteness which is the privilege of the person of leisure.

The art of leisure lies, to me, in the power of absorbing without effort the spirit of one's surroundings ; to look, without speculation, at the sky and the sea ; to become part of a green plain ; to rejoice, with a tranquil mind, in the feast of colour in a bed of flowers. To

75

this end is the good gardener born. The man, who, from a sudden love, stops in his walk to look at a field of Buttercups has no idea of the spiritual advancement he has made.

All this ambles away from the main topic, but so closely does the peace of gardens cling, that thoughts fly over the hedges like bees on the wing and bring back honey from wider pastures and dreams from larger tracts than those the garden itself covers. A man might write a romance of Spain from looking at an Orange.

The Romans, who left an indelible mark on England in their roadways and by their laws, built in this country many villas whose pavements and foundations remain to show us what manner of habitations they were. Besides this we have ample records of the shapes and purposes of these villas, with long accounts of baths, furniture and the like, such as enable us to picture very completely the life of a Roman gentleman exiled to these shores.

Houses, parks, and fields now cover all traces of any gardens there were attached to these Roman villas. Many a man lives over the spot where the hedges and alleys, the flower beds and walks, once delighted those gentlemen who sat drinking Falerian wine poured from old amphoræ dated by the year of the consul. Where sheep now browse gentlemen have sat after a feast of delicacies—Syrian Plums stewed with Pomegranate seeds ; roasted field-fares, fresh Asparagus ; Dates sent from Thebes—and, having eaten, have enjoyed the work of their topiarius, whose skill has cut hedges of Laurel, Box, and Yew into the forms of ships, bears, beasts and birds.

Differing from the Greeks, who were not good gardeners, the Romans, with a skill learnt partly from

Oriental countries, made much of their gardens, and
laid them out with infinite care and arrangement.
They raised their flower-beds in terraces, and edged
them with neat box borders ; they made walks for shade,
and walks for sun ; planted thickets, alleys of fruit
trees, orchards, and Vine pergolas. They had, as a rule,
in larger gardens, a gestatio, a broad pathway in which
they were carried about in litters. They had the
hippodromus, a circus for exercise, which had several
entrances with paths leading to different parts of the
garden.

It is not too much to presume that the Romans, who
spent their lives in our country, and build magnificent
villas for themselves, and brought over all the arts of
their country, brought, also, their methods of gardening,
and planted here as they planted in their villas outside
Rome, all the flowers, fruits and vegetables that the
country would produce.

Tacitus was of the opinion that " the soil and climate
of England was very fit for all kinds of fruit trees,
except Vine and Olive ; and for all kinds of edible
vegetables." In this he was right but for the Vine, which
was planted here in the Third Century, and we know
of vineyards and wine made from them in the Eighth
Century.

Of gardeners there was the topiarius, a fancy gardener,
whose main business it was to be expert on growing,
cutting and clipping trees. The villicus, or viridarius,
who was the real villa gardener, with much the same
duties as our gardener of to-day. The hortulanus is a
later term. And there was the aquarius, a slave whose
duty it was to see that all the garden was provided with
proper aqueducts, and who managed the fountains
which, without doubt, formed a great part in garden
ornament. I imagine, also, that the aquarius would

have control over the supply of hot water which must flow through the green-houses where early fruits and flowers were forced ; such fruits as Winter Grapes, Melons, and Gherkins ; and of flowers, the Rose in particular, for use in garlands and crowns.

Violets and Roses were the principal flowers, being often grown as borders to the beds of vegetables, so that one might find Violets, Onions, Turnips, and Kidney Beans flourishing together.

Besides these flowers there were also the Crocus, Narcissus, Lily, Iris, Hyacinth (the Greek emblem of the dead in memory of the youth killed by Apollo by mistake with a quoit), Poppy, and the bright red Damask Rose and Lupias.

In the orchards of Rome were Cherries, Plums, Quinces, Pomegranates, Peaches, Almonds, Medlars, and Mulberries ; and in the vineyards were thirty varieties of Grapes. Those kinds of fruits which were hardy enough to stand our climate were grown here, and to judge from all account only the Olive failed to meet the test.

Not only were flowers and fruit grown in profusion but Herbs, Asparagus, and Radishes had their place.

Honey, which took a great place in Roman cookery, and in making possets, and in thickening wine, was provided by bees kept especially in apiaries built in sheltered places, with beds of Cytisus, and Thyme and Apiastrum by them. The hives were built of brick or baked dung, and were placed in tiers, the lowest on stone parapets about three feet above the ground ; these parapets being covered with smooth stucco to prevent lizards and insects from entering the hives.

The descriptions by the younger Pliny of his villas and gardens are so delightful in themselves, besides being of great value, that I am going to quote largely from them.

78

THE ROMAN GARDEN IN ENGLAND

The village of Laurentium where Pliny built his villa was on the shores of the Tuscan Sea, and not far from the mouth of the Tiber. The villa was built as a refuge after a hard day's work in Rome, which was only seventeen miles away. "A distance," he says, "which allows us, after we have finished the business of the day, to return thither from town, with the setting sun."

There were two roads from Rome to this villa, the one the Laurentine road—"if you go the Laurentine you must quit the high road at the fourteenth stone "—and the Ostian road, where the branch took place at the eleventh.

After a description of the house and the baths he writes of the garden :

" At no great distance is the tennis-court, so situated, as never to be annoyed by the heat, and to be visited only by the setting sun. At the end of the tennis-court rises a tower, containing two rooms at the top of it, and two again under them ; besides a banqueting room, from whence there is a view of very wide ocean, a very extensive continent, and numberless beautiful villas interspersed upon the shore. Answerable to this is another turret containing, on the top, one single room where we enjoy both the rising and the setting sun. Underneath is a very large store-room for fruit, and a granary, and under these again a dining-room from whence, even when the sea is most tempestuous, we only hear the roaring of it, and that but languidly and at a distance. It looks upon the garden, and the place for exercise which encludes my garden. The whole is encompassed with Box; and where that is wanting with Rosemary ; for Box, when sheltered by buildings, will flourish very well, but wither immediately if exposed to wind and weather, or ever so distantly affected by the moist dews from the sea. The place for exercise

79

surrounds a delicate shady vineyard, the paths of which are easy and soft even to the naked feet.

" The garden is filled with Mulberry and Fig trees ; the soil being propitious to both those kinds of trees, but scarce to any other.

" A dining-room, too remote to view the ocean, commands an object no less agreeable, the prospect of the garden : and at the back of the dining-room are two apartments, whose windows look upon the vestibule of the house ; and upon a fruitery and a kitchen garden. From hence you enter into a covered gallery, large enough to appear a public work. The gallery has a double row of windows on both sides ; in the lower row are several which look towards the sea ; and one on each side towards the garden ; in the upper row there are fewer ; in calm days when there is not a breath of air stirring we open all the windows, but in windy weather we take the advantage of opening that side only which is entirely free from the hurricane. Before the gallery lies a terrace perfumed with Violets. The building not only retains the heat of the sun, and increases it by reflexion, but defends and protects us from the northern blasts."

After a further description of this gallery written with some care, Pliny begins his praise of his garden apartment. No man but a man of true leisure could have dwelt so lovingly on a description of a summer-house. Herrick loved his simple things as much, and sang them tenderly. The small things that come close to us, to keep us warm from all life's disappointments, these are the things our hearts sing out to, these are the things we think of when we are from home. " At the end of the terrace, adjoining to the gallery, is a little garden-apartment, which I own is my delight. In truth it is my mistress : I built it ; and in it is a particular kind of sun-trap which looks on one side towards the terrace, on the other towards the sea, but on both sides has the advantage of the sun. A double door opens into another room, and one of the windows has a full view of the gallery. On the side next the sea, over against the middle wall, is an elegant little closet ; separated only by transparent windows, and a curtain which can be opened or shut at pleasure, from the room just mentioned. It holds a bed and two chairs ; the feet of the bed stand towards the sea, the back towards the house, and one side of it towards some distant woods. So many different views, seen from so many different windows diversify and yet blend the prospect.

" Adjoining to this cabinet is my own constant bed-chamber, where I am never disturbed by the discourse of my servants, the murmurs of the sea, nor the violence of a storm. Neither lightning nor daylight can break in upon me till my own windows are opened. The reason of so perfect and undisturbed a calm here arises from a large void space which is left between the walls of the bedchamber and of the garden ; so that all sound is drowned in the intervening space.

" Close to the bedchamber is a little stove, placed so near a small window of communication that it lets out, or retains, the heat just as we think fit.

" From hence we pass through a lobby into another room, which stands in such a position as to receive the sun, though obliquely, from daybreak till past noon."

There is one thing in this description that is very noteworthy, the absolute content with everything, the lack of any note of grumbling. After all, the pleasures of that garden apartment were very simple ; he took his joy of the sun, the wind, and the distant sound of the sea Heat, light, and the pleasant music of nature ; the bank of Violets near by, the prospect of the villas on the shore glimmmering amidst their greenery in the sun; the songs of birds in the thickets of Myrtle and Rosemary, there made up the fine moments of his life.

Such little houses were copied from the Eastern idea, such as is pointed to several times in the Bible. The Shunamite gives such a house to Elisha :

" Let us make him a little chamber, I pray thee, with walls ; and let us set him there a bed, and a table, and a stool, and a candlestick, that he may turn in thither when he cometh to us."

Whether a Roman living in England ever built himself such a house it is difficult to prove, since, so far as I can find, no remains of such a place are to be seen. But, when one considers the actual evidence of the Roman Occupation, the yields given by the neighbourhoods of Roman cities, the statues, vases, toys, the amphitheatres for cock-fighting, wrestling, and gladiatoral combat, then surely there were gardens of great wonder near to these cities where men like Pliny went to sit in their garden houses and enjoyed the cool of the evening after a day's work.

I have always made it a fancy of mine to suppose such an apartment to have stood on the spot where a garden house I know now stands. I have sat in this little house, a tiny place compared to Pliny's, and pictured to myself the surrounding country as it might have looked under the eyes of our Roman conquerors. Not far distant is a Roman town, outside which is a huge amphitheatre ; the Roman road, via Iceniana, cutting through the western downs and forests. Over this very countryside were villas scattered here and there, bridges, walls, moats and camps. Even to-day, not far away from my summer-house, are two small Roman bridges, over which, in my day-dreams, the previous occupier of the site has often passed.

THE ROMAN GARDEN IN ENGLAND

Here, from this summer-house, I look upon an apiary,
a bed of Violets, a little wood that gives shelter to the
birds, a running stream where trout leap in the pools
My Roman friend, had he built his house here, would
have looked, as I look, at green meadows, and across them
to a wild heath on which rise the very mounds he must
have known, British earthworks, and the heap-up burial
places of great British chiefs.   Round about the house
grow many flowers that would seem homely to my
ghostly friend, Roses, Lilies, Narcissi, Violets, Poppies.
Here he might have sat and contemplated, as Pliny did,
and taken his pleasure of the sun, the wind, the birds.
The sea he could not have heard, since it is eight miles
away, but he could well have seen storms come up over
the western downs, known that the Roman galleys were
seeking shelter in the coves and harbours, and noticed
how the gulls flew screaming inland, and the Egyptian
swallows flew low before the coming tempest.

This house that I know is a simple affair, compared
to the elaborate design of Pliny's ; it is a small thatched
single apartment built in the elbow of the garden wall.
It is not tuned to trap the sun, or dull the sounds of the
violence of the winds, but its solitary window opens wide
to let in the sound of the bees at work, the thrush singing
in the Lilac tree, or tapping his snails on a big stone by the
side of the garden path.   It has a shelf for books, two
chairs, a writing table, and an infinity of those odds and
ends a person collects who deals with bees.   Withal it is
pervaded by a very sweet smell of honey.

Then there are ghosts for company if the books, the
birds, and the bees fail.   There is my Roman to speak
for his villa, for the glories of the town near by.   There
is the British chieftain whose mound is not two miles
away, a mound where his charred ashes lie, but the urn
that held them is on a shelf overhead.   There are Saxons

who have trod this very ground, and Danes and Normans, men also from Anjou, Gascony, and Maine, and a host of others. Then there are the flowers themselves with romances every one.

If I have a mind to following fancy and turn this into a veritable Roman garden, I can link my fancy with Pliny's facts and see how it would have been ordered and arranged. I can see the villa portico with its terrace in front of it adorned with statues and edged with Box. Below here is a gravel walk on each side of which are figures of animals cut in Box. Then there is the circus at the end of a broad path, where my Roman friend could exercise himself on horseback. Round about the circus are sheared dwarf trees, and clipped Box hedges. On the outside of this is a lawn, smooth and green. Then comes my summer-house shaded with Plane trees, with a marble fountain that plays on the roots of the trees and the grass round them. There would be a walk near by covered with Vines, and ended by an Ivy-covered wall. Several alleys (my imagination has traced their courses) wind in and out to meet in the end of a series of straight walks divided by grass plots, or Box trees cut into a thousand shapes; some of letters forming my Roman's name; others the name of his gardener. In these are mixed small pyramid Apple trees; "and now and then (to follow Pliny's plan) you met, on a sudden, with a spot of ground, wild and uncultivated, as if transplanted hither on purpose." Everywhere are marble or stone seats, little fountains, arbours covered with Vines, and facing beds of Roses, or Violets, or Herbs, and always is to be heard the pleasant murmur of water " conveyed through pipes by the hand of the artificer."

The more I think of it the more I see how exactly the garden I know fulfils this purpose. Except for a greater, a far greater display of flowers, Pliny would be quite at home here. There is an abundance of water; the very site for the horse course; winding alleys, straight paths, and several pergolas for Roses.

A noticeable thing in the planning of a Roman garden, and one that is too often absent from our own, is the great attention paid to the value of water. In many places where there is an abundant supply of water, with streams running close by, or even through the garden, we find no attempt made to use the value of water either decoratively or for useful purposes. We are apt to dispose our gardens for the purposes of large collections of flowers, whereas the Roman with his small store of them was forced to bring every aid to bear on varying his garden, such as seats, fountains, and little artificial brooks. The cost, even in small gardens, of arranging a decorative effect of water, where water is plentiful, would not amount to so very much, and in many cases would be a great saving of labour. We use wells to some extent, and, to my mind, a properly-built well-head, with a roof and posts, and seats, is one of the most beautiful garden ornaments we can have.

The well-head itself should be built of brick raised about eighteen inches above the ground, and should be at least fourteen inches broad in the shelf, so that the buckets have ample room in which to stand. The coil and windlass are better if they are both simple, and of good timber. Round this a brick path, two feet broad, should be laid. Over all a roof of red tiles supported on square wooden posts or brick pillars, would give shade to the well, and to a seat of plain design that should be placed against the outer edge of the brick path. And if beds of flowers were set about it all, as I have seen done, and well done, in a cottage garden in Kent, the effect is quaint and beautiful.

85

THE CHARM OF GARDENS

I have no doubt that in Roman England such wells were built where the supply of water was not equal to great distribution. But it is amazing to think that such a tiny village as Laurentium, where Pliny had one of his villas outside Rome, held three Inns, in each of which were baths always heated and ready for travellers, and that it has taken us until the present day to bring the bath into the ordinary house.

Naturally, when one casts one's eyes over a picture of a Roman garden in England, and compares it with a garden of to-day, the very first thing we find missing is that mass of colour and that wonderful variety of bloom that constitutes the apex of modern gardening. Where they were surprised, or gave themselves sudden shocks to the eye, it was by means of little grottos, fountains, vistas at the ends of long alleys, statues in a wild part of a garden, or unexpected seats commanding a prospect opened out by an arrangement of the trees. We prepare for ourselves wildernesses in which the Spring shall paint her wonderful picture of Anemones, Daffodils, Crocuses, and such flowers ; where Blue Bells and Primroses, Ragged Robin, and Foxgloves hold us by their vivid colour. Our scarlet armies of Geranium, our banks of purple Asters, or the flaming panoplies of Roses with which we illuminate our gardens would seem to the Roman something wonderful and strange. Yet, in a sense, his taste was more subtle. He held green against green, a bed of Herbs, the occasional jewel of a clump of Violets, more to his manner of liking. And he arranged his garden so as to contain as many varieties of walks as possible.

In the evenings now, when I am, by chance, staying in the house whose garden holds that summer-house I love, I can see my old Roman of my dreams wandering over his estate, and I almost feel his presence near me as

86

his ghost sits on the wooden seat by the lawn and his eyes seem to peer across the meadows back to where Rome herself lies over the eastern hills. An exile, buried far from Rome, his spirit seems to hover here as if he could not sleep in peace away from the warm, sweet Italy of his birth.

II

ST. FIACRE, PATRON SAINT OF GARDENERS
AND CAB-DRIVERS

GARDENERS who, to a man, are dedicated to peaceful
and meditative pursuits, should care to know of the story
of Saint Fiacre, the Irish Prince who turned hermit, and
after his death was hailed Patron of Gardeners.

He left Ireland, says the story, at that time when a
missionary zeal was sending Irish monks the length and
breadth of Europe. As Saint Pol left Britain and slew
the Dragon on the Isle of Batz ; Saint Gall drove the
spirits of flood across the Lake of Constance ; Saint
Columban founded monasteries in Burgundy and the
Apennines, so did Saint Fiacre leave his native land and
take himself to France, and there by a miracle enlarge
the space of his garden.

At Meaux, on the river Marne, near Paris, the Bishop
Saint Faron had founded a new monastery in the woods
and called it the Monastery of Saint Croix. To this
monastery came the son of the Irish King, and made his
vows. It was early days in Europe, for Saint Fiacre
died in or about the year 670, and it is almost impossible
to imagine the perils and discomforts of his journey, for
in Britain and Gaul fighting was going on, roads were bad
and unsafe, the sea had to be crossed in an open boat.

But these Celts, driven west by war, now began to
make their own war on Europe, not with sword and
shield and battle-cry, but with pilgrim's staff, and reed

pen, and the device of Christ on their hearts.   Illumination, one of the marvels of monkish accomplishment, was spread throughout Europe by bands of Irish monks, who, taking the wonderful traditions of such work as " The Book of Kells," and those works written and illuminated at Lindisfarne, went their ways from country to country spreading their culture as well as their message.

Saint Fiacre stayed a certain time in the monastery until, indeed, the voice within him calling for more solitude and for another mode of life, forced him to go to the Bishop.   To him he spoke of his vocation, of those feelings within him that prompted him to become a hermit.

The good Bishop seeing in Fiacre a good intention, and perceiving doubtless the holy nature of the monk, granted him a space on his own domain, some way from the monastery, on the edge of the woods and the plain of Brie.   To this place the monk repaired and began the great work of his life.

Now it is not easy for the best of men at the best of times to live solitary in a wood without becoming something of a self-conscious or morbid person.   Not so with these old hermits.   They seemed to have the grace of such excessive spirituality as to have been uplifted above ordinary men, and to have lost all sense of loneliness in conversation with the Saints, and in communion with God.

What finer means of reaching this exalted condition than by labouring to make a garden in the wilderness ? Saint Fiacre cleared a space in the woods with his own hands, and in this space he built an oratory to Our Lady, and a hut by it wherein he dwelt.   All must have been of the most primitive order ; one of those beehive shaped buildings, such as still remain in Ireland, for the oratory, fashioned out of stones and mud in what is called rag-work, and most probably roofed with turf.

After the work of building he began to make his garden. It is evident that his clearing was not near the river as the fountain or well from which he drew his water is still to be seen and it is a considerable distance away.

Imagine the solitary life of this priest gardener, whose food depended entirely on the produce of the ground. To any man the silence of the woods holds a mysterious calm, a weird, haunting uneasiness. To dwellers in woods, after a time, the silence becomes full of friendly voices; the fall of Acorns; the crackling of twigs as a wild animal forces a passage through the undergrowth; the snap of trees in the frost; the shuffling of birds getting ready for the night. But here, in the wild woods of Meaux in those early times, wolves, bears, wild boars lived.

It is possible to imagine the Saint on his knees at night, the trees, dark masses round his garden, a heaven above him pitted with stars, the smoke of his breath as he prays rising like incense. And, as has been known to be the case, all wild animals fearless of him, and friendly to him in whom they see, by instinct, one who will do them no harm. As Saint Jerome laid down with the lions, as Saint Francis spoke with Brother Wolf, and Sister Lark, so Saint Fiacre must have spoken with his friends, the beasts. In the heart of a gardener lies something to which all wild nature responds.

But consider a man of that time alone in the wood, at that time when men knew so little and whose lives were full of superstitious guesses at scientific facts. And think how much more full of dread Fiacre must have been than an ordinary man, since he was one of a nation to whom fairies and goblins of every kind are daily actualities. Think of the Saint seeing his own face daily reflected in the well as he drew his water ; think of the mysterious quality of water in lonely wells when it seems now to be troubled by unseen hands, now to lift a clear smiling face to the sky. He must be a mystic and a man filled with a simple goodness who can garden in a wilderness like this.

One can picture him seated at the door of his hut eating his Acorn mash or Herb soup after a day's work and prayer. A stout wooden spade rests by his side, the shaft of Oak worn smooth by his hands. In front of him what labours show in the ground ! Huge stumps of trees that have been uprooted and dragged away ; herbs he has tried to grow showing green in the heavy soil ; wild flowers sweeting the air ; here the beginnings of a vineyard ; there the first blades of a patch of Wheat, or Oats.

In various parts of Europe were other Irish people at work sweetening the soil. Saint Gobhan near Laon, Saint Etto, at Dompierre, Saint Caidoc and Saint Fricor in Picardy, and Saint Judoc also there, Saint Fursey, at Lagny, six miles north of Paris ; and a daughter of an Irish king, Saint Dympna, at Gheel, in Belgium. These are but a few of the Irish who ventured forth to save the world. Beyond all of these does Saint Fiacre appeal to us who love our gardens.

Self-denial has been called the luxury of the Saints, yet the phrase-maker would seem to such denials of unessentials as rich foods and wines, and mortifications of the flesh which a man may choose to do without any suggestion of Saintship. Here, in Saint Fiacre, we have a man whose process of purification was symbolised by his work. The uprooting of trees, the uprooting of a thousand superstitious ideas ; the purifying of the soil, the cleansing of his heart ; the growing of food, the sustenance for his spirit besides his body.

He leaves his native land, he becomes monk, hermit, gardener. He dwells in the wilds of a forest, one man, alone, doing no great deed one might imagine that would cause his fame to travel, living his quiet simple life shut right away from the world by leagues of forest, more buried than a man in the wilderness. For cathedral, the depth of his woods, the aisles of great trees, the tracery and windows made by boughs and leaves. For choir, the birds. He was, one would think, so utterly alone, that no step but his own ever broke the silence of the woodland glades ; so isolated that no human voice but his own ever penetrated the brakes and thickets. Yet he became known.

Doubtless some hunter, a wild man, to whom the tracks in the forest were as roads, coming one day through the woods after game, burst into the clearing, and stood amazed, paused suspicious, wondering to see the little oratory, the hut, the garden all about. The hunter casts his keen eyes about, here and there, alert, scenting danger, eyeing the new place with anxious wonder, holding his spear in readiness. Then comes the Saint from his hut and calls him brother, bids him put down his spear, sit and eat.

The hunter goes ; a swineherd, seeking lost droves of pigs turned loose to fatten on the acorns, comes across the place. The news filters through the country, reaches the huddled villages by the river, reaches the dwellers in the hills, the people of the forest. They come to look, to stare, to be amazed. To each Saint Fiacre offers his hospitality.

As men, drawn irresistibly by a strong personality, will throng towards a well whose water is supposed to contain some virtue, or a stone to touch which restores

lost friends, so they came to test the holiness of this
man of the woods, and found him good, and true, and
full of peace. And they marvelled to find a garden in
the wood, and, being entreated, eat of its produce, and
heard the holy man preach, and saw him heal. Then
the Saint was forced to build another hut for those of
his visitors who came from far to consult him, and, as
the crowds grew greater he was forced to go to the Bishop
to ask for more land.

Saint Faron, the Bishop of Meaux, to whom all the
forest belonged, knew his man. One can imagine two
such men leading lofty and spiritual lives meeting in the
monastery. I like to think of the Bishop as one of those
thin men full of years, with a skin like parchment, his
holiness shining out of his eyes, a man whose quiet
voice, tuned to the silence of the monastery, breathes
peace. And Fiacre, bronzed with the open air, rough
with labour, with the curious eyes of the mystic, eyes
that looked as if they had pierced the veil of a mystery,
standing before his Bishop asking for his grant of land.

Coming from the depths of the heavy wood into the
town, leaving the silence of his forest for the noise of the
place, he must have felt strange. Those who met him
were, I am sure, conscious of the atmosphere he carried
with him, the envelope all lonely men wear, the curious
reserve common to all dwellers in woods, and wilds.

The Bishop consented to the demand, and gave him
his desire after a curious manner. Perhaps to test
this hermit whose fame had already spread so far,
perhaps to see how real were the stories he must have
heard of his spiritual son, this holy gardener, he granted
him as much land as he could enclose with his spade in
one day.

Back went Saint Fiacre to his forest clearing, to his
friends the birds, his bubbling wells, his aisles of trees,

his garden, now well grown, and, breaking a stick he marked out far and wide the space of land he needed, more than any man could in one day enclose with any spade. And after that into the little oratory he went and prayed for help.

You may be sure every movement of this was carefully observed. A woman envied him and spied on these proceedings. I take it she was some woman to whom, before the Saint grew famous, the peasants came for spells and simples, a wise woman, a witch, whose reputation was at stake.

The Saint's prayer was answered. The woman, evil report on her tongue, made her journey to the Bishop of Meaux, and accused Fiacre of magic, of dealings with the Devil. Roused by the report, the Bishop came to see the Saint and saw all that had happened. In one day all the wide space Fiacre had marked out had been enclosed. After that the oratory was denied to all women. Even as late as 1641, nearly a thousand years after his death, when Anne of Austria visited his shrine in the Cathedral of Meaux she did not enter the Chapel but remained outside the grating. It was the legend, handed down all that time, that any woman who entered there would go blind or mad.

Where the Saint had dug his solitary garden, and on the site of his cell a great Benedictine Priory was built in after years, where his body was kept and did many wonders of healing, especially in the cure of a certain fleshy tumour, which they called " le fie de St. Fiacre." After many years, in the beginning of the seventeenth century, his body was removed to the Cathedral at Meaux.

So it may be seen for how good a cause he became known as Patron of Gardeners, and it must now be shown why he is called the Patron of Cab Drivers. In

94

St. FIACRE

1640 a man of the name of Sauvage started an establish-
ment in Paris from which he let out carriages for hire.
He took a house for this business in the Rue St. Martin,
and the house was known as the Hotel de St. Fiacre,
and there was a figure of the Saint over the doorway.

All the coaches plying from here began to be called,
for short, fiacres, and the drivers placed images of the
Saint on their carriages, and claimed him as their patron.

There is a Pardon of St. Fiacre in Brittany ; and there
are churches and altars to him all over France.

III

EVELYN'S "SYLVA"

On my table, as I write, is the copy of "Sylva" that John Evelyn himself gave to Sir Robert Morray, and in which he wrote in ink that is now faded and brown, as are his own autograph corrections in the text,

"—from his most humble servant, Evelyn."

The title page runs thus :

SYLVA,

or a Discourse of

FOREST-TREES,

AND THE

Propagation of Timber

In His MAJESTIES Dominions

By J. E. Esq ;

As it was Delivered in the ROYAL SOCIETY the XVth of October CIƆIƆCLXII. upon Occasion of certain Quaeries Propounded to that Illustrious Assembly, by the Honorable the Principal Officers, and Commissioners of the Navy.

To which is annexed

POMONA or, An Appendix concerning Fruit-Trees in relation to CIDER ;

The Making and several ways of Ordering it.

Published by the express Order of the ROYAL SOCIETY

EVELYN'S "SYLVA"

ALSO

KALENDARIUM HORTENSE; Or, ye Gard'ners Almanac;
Directing what he is to do Monethly throughout the year.

—Tibi res antiquæ laudis et artis
Ingredior, tantos ausus recludere fonteis.   *Virg.*

LONDON: Printed by Jo. Martyn, and Ja. Allestry, Printers
to the Royal Society, and are to be sold at their Shop at the
Bell in S. Paul's Church-yard;
MDCLXIV.

This book was the first ever printed for the Royal
Society, and contains, as may be seen, a practically complete record of seventeenth century planting and gardening, thus having an unique interest for all who follow the
craft.

John Evelyn, from the day he began his lessons
under the Friar in the porch of Wotton Church, was a
curious observer of men and things, but especially was
he devoted to all manners and styles of gardening.

Nothing was too small, too trivial to escape his notice;
from the weather-cocks on the trees near Margate—put
there on the days the farmers feasted their servants, to
the interest he found in watching the first man he ever
saw drink coffee.

The positions he held under Charles II. and James II.
were many and varied, yet he found time to collect
samples in Venice, and travel extensively, to write a Play,
a treatise called: "Mundus Muliebris, or the Ladies'
Dressing Room, Unlocked," and a pamphlet, called
"Tyrannus, or the Mode," in which he sought to make
Charles II. dress like a Persian, and succeeded in so
doing.

But above all these things he held his chiefest pleasure
in seeing and talking of the arrangement of gardens,
passing on this love to his son John, who, when a boy of
fifteen, at Trinity College, Oxford, translated "Rapin,

97

or Gardens," the second book of which his father included in his second edition of " Sylva."

His Majesty Charles II., to whom the " Sylva " is
dedicated, was a monarch to whom justice has never
been properly done. He is represented by pious but
inaccurate historians, those men who for many years
gave a false character of jovial good nature to that gross
thief and sacrilegious monster, Henry VIII., as a King
who spent most of his time in the Playhouse, or in talking
trivialities with gay ladies, and in making witty remarks
to all and sundry in his Court. The side of him that took
interest in shipbuilding, navigation, astronomy, in the
founding of the Royal Society, in the advancement of Art,
in the minor matters of flower gardening and bee-keeping
is nearly always suppressed. It was largely through his
interest in this volume of Evelyn's that the Royal forests
were properly replanted ; and it was in a great measure
due to Royal interest that the parks and estates of the
noblemen of England became famous in after years for
their beautiful timber.

In that part of the " Sylva " dealing with forest trees,
there were a hundred hints to all lovers of nature and of
gardens, for your good gardener is a man very near in his
nature to a good strong tree, and loves to observe the
play of light and shade in the branches of those that give
shade to his garden walks.

Evelyn tells us how the Ash is the sweetest of forest
fuelling, and the fittest for Ladies' Chambers, also for the
building of Arbours, the staking of Espaliers, and the
making of Poles. The white rot of it makes a ground for
the Sweet-powder used by gallants. He tries to intro-
duce the Chestnut as food, saying how it is a good, lusty
and masculine food for Rustics ; and commenting on the
fact that the best tables in France and Italy make them
a service. He tells us how the water in which Walnut

husks and leaves are boiled poured on the carpet of walks and bowling-greens infallibly kills the worms without hurting the grass. That, by the way, is a matter for discussion among gardeners, seeing that some say that the movements of worms from below the surface to their cast on the lawn lets air among the grass roots and is good for them.

He tells us how the Horn-beam makes the stateliest hedge for long garden walks. He advises us how to make wine of the Birch, Ash, Elder, Oak, Crab and Bramble. He praises the Service-Tree, and the Eugh, and the Jasmine, saying of this last how one sorry tree in Paris where they grow " has been worth to a poor woman, near twenty shillings a year."

All this and much besides of diverting and instructive reading, varied with remarks on the gardens of his friends and acquaintances, as when he " cannot but applaud the worthy Industry of old *Sir Harbotle Grimstone*, who (I am told) from a very small *Nursery of Acorns* which he sowed in the neglected corners of his ground, did draw forth such numbers of *Oaks* of competent growth ; as being planted about his *Fields* in even and uniform rows, about one hundred foot from the *Hedges* ; bush'd and well water'd till they had sufficiently fix'd themselves, did wonderfully improve both the beauty, and the value of his *Demeasnes*," for the honour and glory of filling England with fine trees and gardens to improve, what he calls—the Landskip.

The exigencies of the present moment when Imperial Finance threatens to tax all good parks and orchards out of existence, and to make all fine flower gardens out of use, except to the enormously wealthy, makes the " Gard'ners Calendar " all the more interesting as showing what manner of flowers, fruits, and vegetables were in use in the Seventeenth Century, and the means employed to grow and preserve them.

Then, as now, there was a danger of over cultivation of certain plants and flowers, so that a man might have more pride in the number and curiosity of his flowers, than in the beauty and colour of them. It is a certain fault in modern gardeners that they do not study the grouping and massing of colours, but do, more generally, take pride in over-large specimens, great collections, and rare varieties. But this age and that are times of collecting, of connoisseurship, ages that produce us great art of their own but have an extraordinary knowledge of the arts and devices of the past. Not that I would decry the friendly competitions of this and that man to grow rare rock plants, or bloom exotics the one against another, but I do most certainly prefer a rivalry in producing beautiful effects of colour ; and love better to see a great mass of Roses growing free than to see one poor tree twisted into the semblance of a flowering parasol as men now use in many of the small climbing Roses.

To the end that gardeners and lovers of gardens may know how those past gardeners treated their fruits and flowers, I give the whole of Evelyn's "Gard'ners Calendar," than which no more complete account of gardens of that time exists.

It would be as well to note, before arriving at our Seventeenth Century Calendar, how the art of gardening had grown in England after the time of the Romans.

From the time that every sign of the Roman occupation had been wiped out to the beginning of the thirteenth century, gardens as we know them to-day did not exist. The first attempts at gardens within castle walls were little plots of herbs and shrubs with a few trees of Costard Apples. It appears that all those plants and flowers the Romans cultivated had been lost, and that

with the sterner conditions of living all such arrange
ments as arbours of cut Yew trees, or elaborate Box-
edged paths had completely vanished. Certainly they
did have arbours for shade, but of a simple kind and quite
unlike the elaborate garden houses the Romans built.

There were vineyards and wine made from them as
early as the Eighth Century, and in the reign of Edward
the Third wine was made at Windsor Castle by Stephen
of Bourdeaux. The Cherry trees brought here by the
Romans had quite died out and were not recovered
until Harris, Henry the Eighth's Irish fruiterer, grew
them again at Sittingbourne. In the Twelfth Century
flower gardening again came in, and within the castle
walls pleasant gardens were laid out with little avenues
of fruit trees, and neat beds of flowers. Of the fruit
trees there was the Costard Apple, the only Apple of that
time, from which great quantities of cider—that
" good-natured and potable liquor "—was made. There
was the great Wardon Pear, from which the celebrated
Wardon pies were made ; they were Winter Pears from
a stock originally cultivated by those great horti-
culturists the Cistercian monks of Wardon in Bedford-
shire. Then there was also the Quince, called a Coyne,
the Medlar, and I believe the Mulberry, or More tree.
In the borders, Strawberries, Raspberries, Barberries
and Currants were grown, that is in a well-stocked
garden such as the Earl of Lincoln had in Holborn in
1290. Then there was a plot set aside as a Physic
garden where herbs grew and salads of Rocket, Lettuce,
Mustard, Watercress, and Hops. In one place, probably
overlooking the pond or fountain which was the centre
of such gardens, was an arbour, and walks and smaller
gardens were screened off by wattle hedges. In that
part of the garden devoted to flowers were Roses, Lilies,
Sunflowers, Violets, Poppies, Narcissi, Pervinkes or

Periwinkles. Lastly, and most important was the Clove Pink, Orgilly-flower, a variety of Wallflower then called Bee-flower. Add to this an apiary and you have a complete idea of the mediæval garden.

Later, in the Fifteenth Century came a new feature into the garden, a mound built in the centre for the view, made sometimes of earth, but very often of wood raised up as a platform, and having gaily carved and painted stairways. These, with butts for archery, and bowling-greens, and a larger variety of the old kinds of flowers, showed the principal difference.

We come now to the gardens of the Sixteen Century, when flower gardening was extremely popular. Spenser and the other poets are always describing the beauties of flowers, and from these and old Herbals, from Bacon, Shakespeare and other writers of that time, we are able to see how, slowly but surely, the art of flower growing had advanced. The gardens were very exact and formal, and were divided in geometrical patterns, and grew large " seats " of Violets, Penny Royal, and Mint as well as other herbs. Above all, a new addition to the mounds, archery butts and bowling-greens, was the maze which had a place in every proper garden of the Elizabethans.

The first garden where flower growing was taken really seriously belonged to John Parkinson, a London apothecary who had a garden in Long Acre. Great importance was given to smell, as is highly proper, and flower gardens were bordered with Thyme, Marjoram and Lavender. Highly-scented flowers were the most prized, and for this reason the prime favourite the Carnation, was more grown than any other flower. Of this there were fifty distinct varieties of every shape and size, including the famous large Clove Pink, the golden coloured Sops-in-Wine.

102

With the increase in the variety of the Rose, of which
about thirty kinds were known, came the fashion,
quickly universal, of keeping potpourri of dried Rose
leaves, many of which were imported from the East,
from whence, years before, had come quantities of Roses
to supply the demand in Winter in Rome.

As the fashion for growing flowers increased so, also,
did the efforts of gardeners to procure new and rare
flowers from foreign countries, and soon the Fritillary,
Tulip and Iris were extensively cultivated, and were
treated with extraordinary care.

Following this came the rage for Anemones and
Ranunculi, in which people endeavoured to excel over
their friends. And after that came in small Chrysanthemums, Lilac or Blue Pipe tree, Lobelia, and the
Acacia tree.

It will be seen that within quite a short space of time
the old garden containing few flowers, and only those
as a rule that had some medicinal properties, vanished
before a perfect orgy of colour and wealth of varieties ;
and that gardening for pleasure gave the people a new
and fascinating occupation. The rage for Anemones
and for the different kinds of Ranunculus developed
until in the late Seventeenth Century the madness,
for it was nothing else, for Tulip collecting came in,
to give place still later to the Rose, and in our day only
to be equalled by the collection of Chrysanthemums
and Orchids.

The best books previous to Evelyn's " Sylva " are
Gervase Markham's " Country House-Wife's Garden,"
(1617), and John Parkinson's " Paradisus in Sole "
(1629).

One word more on the subject of flower mania. The
rage for the Tulip that attacked both English and
Dutch in the late Seventeenth Century is one of the

most peculiar things in the history of gardening. The Tulip is really a Persian flower, the shape of it suggesting the name, thoulyban, a Persian turban. It was introduced into England about 1577, by way of Germany, having been brought there by the German Ambassador from Constantinople. By the Seventeenth Century there had developed such a passion for this flower that it led to wreck and ruin of rich men who paid fabulous sums for the bulbs, a single bulb being sold for a fortune. One bulb of the Semper Augustus was sold for four thousand six hundred florins, a new carriage, a pair of grey horses, and complete harness. So great did the business in Tulips become that every Dutch town had special Tulip exchanges, and there speculators assembled and bid away vast sums to acquire rare kinds. The mania lasted about three years, and was only finally stopped by the Government.

PART III

KALENDARIUM HORTENSE

KALENDARIUM HORTENSE:

OR THE

GARD'NERS ALMANAC;

DIRECTING WHAT HE IS TO DO

MONETHLY

THROUGHOUT THE

YEAR

1664

JANUARY.

To be done

In the Orchard, and Olitory Garden.

Trench the ground, and make it ready for the Spring : prepare also soil, and use it where you have occasion : Dig Borders, &c., uncover as yet Roots of Trees, where Ablaqueation is requisite.

Plant Quick-Sets, and Transplant Fruit-trees, if not finished : Set Vines ; and begin to prune the old : Prune the branches of Orchard-fruit-trees ; Nail, and trim your Wall-fruit, and Espaliers.

Cleanse Trees of Moss, &c., the weather moist.

Gather Cyons for graffs before the buds sprout ; and about the later end, Graff them in the Stock : Set Beans, Pease, etc.

Sow also (if you please) for early Colly-flowers.

Sow Chevril, Lettuce, Radish, and other (more delicate) Saleting ; if you will raise in the Hot-bed.

In over wet, or hard weather, cleanse, mend, sharpen and prepare garden-tools.

Turn up your Bee-hives, and sprinkle them with a little warm and sweet Wort ; do it dextrously.

Fruits in Prime, or Yet Lasting.

APPLES.

Kentish-pepin, Russet-pepin, Golden-pepin, French pepin, Kirton-pepin, Holland-pepin, John-apple, Winter-queening, Mari-gold, Harvey-apple, Pome-water, Pomeroy, Golden-Doucet, Reineting, Loues-pearmain, Winter-Pearmain, etc.

PEARS.

Winter-husk (bakes well), Winter-Norwich (excellently baked), Winter-Bergamot, Winter-Bon-crestien, both Mural: the great Surrein, etc.

JANUARY.

To be done

IN THE PARTERRE, AND FLOWER GARDEN.

Set up your Traps for Vermin; especially in your Nurseries of Kernels and Stones, and amongst your Bulbous-roots: About the middle of this month, plant your Anemony-roots, which will be secure of, without covering, or farther trouble: Preserve from too great and continuing Rains (if they happen), Snow and Frost, your choicest Anemonies, and Ranunculus's sow'd in September, or October for earlier Flowers: Also your Carnations, and such seeds as are in peril of being wash'd out, or over chill'd and frozen; covering them with Mats and shelter, and striking off the Snow where it lies too weighty; for it certainly rots, and bursts your early-set Anemonies and Ranunculus's, etc., unless planted now in the Hot-bed; for now is the Season, and they will flower even in London. Towards the end, earth-up, with fresh and light mould, the Roots of those Auriculas which the frosts may have uncovered; filling up the chinks about the sides of the Pots where your choicest are set: but they need not be hous'd; it is a hardy Plant.

FLOWERS IN PRIME, OR YET LASTING.

Winter Aconite, some Anemonies, Winter Cyclamen,

THE CHARM OF GARDENS

Black Hellebor, Beumal-Hyacinth, Oriental-Jacynth, Levantine-Narcissus, Hepatica, Prime-Roses, Laurustinus, Mezereon, Praecoce Tulips, etc., especially if raised in the (Hot-bed).

NOTE.

That both these Fruits and Flowers are more early, or tardy, both as to their prime Seasons of eating, and perfection of blowing, according as the soil, and situation, are qualified by Nature or Accident.

NOTE ALSO

That in this Recension of Monethly Flowers, it is to be understood for the whole period that any flower continues, from its first appearing, to its final withering.

FEBRUARY.

To be done

In the Orchard, and Olitory Garden.

Prime Fruit-trees, and Vines, as yet. Remove graffs of former year graffing. Cut and lay Quick-sets. Yet you may Prune some Wall-fruit (not finish'd before) the most tender and delicate : But be exceedingly careful of the now turgid buds and bearers ; and trim up your Palisade Hedges, and Espaliers. Plant Vines as yet, and the Shrubs, Hops, etc.

Set all sorts of kernels and stony seeds. Also sow Beans, Pease, Radish, Parsnips, Carrots, Onions, Garlick, etc., and Plant Potatoes in your worst ground.

Now is your Season for Circumposition by Tubs, Baskets of Earth, and for laying of Branches to take Root. You may plant forth your Cabbage-plants.

Rub Moss off your Trees after a soaking Rain, and scrape and cleanse them of Cankers, etc., draining away the wet (if need require) from the too much moistened Roots, and earth up those Roots of your Fruit-trees, if any were uncover'd. Cut off the webs of Caterpillars, etc. (from the Tops of Twigs and Trees) to burn. Gather Worms in the evenings after Rain.

Kitchen-Garden herbs may now be planted, as Parsly, Spinage, and other hardy Pot-herbs. Towards the middle of later end of this Moneth, till the Sap rises briskly, Graff in the Cleft, and so continue till the last of March ; they will hold Apples, Pears, Cherries, Plums, etc. Now also plant out your Colly-flowers

111

to have early; and begin to make your Hot-bed for the first Melons and Cucumbers; but trust not altogether to them. Sow Asparagus. Lastly,

Half open your passages for the Bees, or a little before (if weather invite); but continue to feed weak Stocks, etc.

FRUITS IN PRIME, OR YET LASTING.
APPLES.

Kentish, Kirton, Russet, Holland Pepins; Deuxans, Winter Queening, Harvey, Pome-water, Pomeroy, Golden Doucet, Reineting, Loues Pearmain, Winter Pearmain, etc.

PEARS.

Bon-crestien of Winter, Winter Poppering, Little Dagobert, etc.

FEBRUARY.

To be done

IN THE PARTERRE, AND FLOWER GARDEN.

Continue Vermine Trapps, etc.

Sow Alaternus seeds in Cases, or open beds; cover them with thorns, that the Poultry scratch them not out.

Now and then air your Carnations, in warm days especially, and mild showers.

Furnish (now towards the end) your Aviarys with Birds before they couple, etc.

112

KALENDARIUM HORTENSE

FLOWERS IN PRIME, OR YET LASTING.

Winter Aconite, single Anemonies, and some double, Tulips praecoce, Vernal Crocus, Black Hellebore, single Hepatica, Persian Iris, Leucoium, Dens Caninus, three leav'd, Vernal Cyclamen, white and red. Yellow Violets with large leaves, early Daffodils, etc.

MARCH.

To be done

In the Orchard, and Olitory Garden.

Yet Stercoration is seasonable, and you may plant what trees are left, though it be something of the latest, unless in very backward or moist places.

Now is your chiefest and best time for raising on the Hot-bed Melons, Cucumbers, Gourds, etc., which about the sixth, eighth or tenth day will be ready for the seeds ; and eight days after prick them forth at distances, according to the method, etc.

If you have them later, begin again in ten or twelve days after the first, and so a third time, to make Experiments.

Graff all this Moneth, unless the Spring prove extraordinary forwards.

You may as yet cut Quick-sets, and cover such Tree-roots as you laid bare in Autumn.

Slip and set Sage, Rosemary, Lavender, Thyme, etc.

Sow in the beginning Endive, Succory, Leeks, Radish, Beets, Chard-Beet, Scorzonera, Parsnips, Skirrets, Parsley, Sorrel, Buglos, Borrage, Chevril, Sellery, Smalladge, Alisanders, etc. Several of which continue many years without renewing, and are most of them to be blanch'd by laying them under litter and earthing up.

Sow also Lettuce, Onions, Garlick, Okach, Parslan, Turneps (to have early) monethly, Pease, etc. these annually.

114

KALENDARIUM HORTENSE

Transplant the Beet-chard which you sow'd in August to have most ample Chards. Sow also Carrots, Cabbages, Cresses, Fennel, Marjoram, Basil, Tobacco, etc. And transplant any sort of Medicinal Hearbs.

Mid-March dress up and string your Strawberry-beds, and uncover your Asparagus, spreading and loosening the Mould about them, for their more easy penetrating. Also you may transplant Asparagus roots to make new Beds.

By this time your Bees sit; keep them close Night and Morning, if the weather prove ill. Turn your Fruit in the Room where it lies, but open not yet the windows.

Fruits in Prime, or Yet Lasting.

Apples.

Golden Duchess (Doucet), Pepins, Reineting, Loues Pearmain, Winter Pearmain, John-Apple, etc.

Pears.

Later Bon-crestien, Double Blossom Pear, etc.

MARCH.

To be done

In the Parterre, and Flower Garden.

Stake and binde up your weakest Plants and Flowers against the Windes, before they come too fiercely, and in a moment prostrate a whole year's labour.

Plant Box, etc., in Parterres. Sow Pinks, Sweet Williams, and Carnations, from the middle to the end of this Moneth. Sow Pine kernels, Firr-seeds, Bays, Alatirnus, Phillyrea, and most perennial Greens, etc. Or you may stay till somewhat later in the Moneth. Sow

115

Auricula seeds in pots or cases, in fine willow earth, a little loamy ; and place what you sow'd in October now in the shade and water it.

Plant some Anemony roots to bear late, and successively : especially in, and about London, where the Smoak is anything tolerable ; and if the Season be very dry, water them well once in two or three days. Fibrous roots may be transplanted about the middle of this Moneth ; such as Hepatica's, Primeroses, Auricula's, Camomile, Hyacinth, Tuberose, Matricaria, Hellebor, and other Summer Flowers ; and towards the end Convolvulus, Spanish or ordinary Jasmine.

Towards the middle or latter end of March sow on the Hot-bed such Plants as are late-bearing Flowers or Fruit in our Climate ; as Balsamine, and Balsamummas, Pomum Onions, Datura, Aethispic Apples, some choice Amaranthmus, Dactyls, Geraniums, Hedysarum Clipeatum, Humble, and Sensitive Plants, Lenticus, Myrtleberries (steep'd awhile), Capsicum Indicum, Canna Indica, Flos Africanus, Minabile Peruvian, Nasturtium Ind., Indian Phaseoli, Volubilis, Myrrh, Carrots, Manacoe, fine flos Passionis and the like rare and exotic plants which are brought us from hot countries.

Note.—That the Nasturtium Ind., African Marygolds, Volubilis and some others, will come(though not altogether so forwards) in the Cold-bed without Art. But the rest require much and constant heat, and therefore several Hot-beds, till the common earth be very warm by the advance of the Sun, to bring them to a due stature, and perfect their Seeds.

About the expiration of this Moneth carry into the shade such Auriculas, Seedlings or Plants as are for their choiceness reserv'd in Pots.

Transplant also Carnation seedlings, giving your layers fresh earth, and setting them in the shade for a week,

116

then likewise cut off all the sick and infected leaves.

Now do the farewell-frosts, and Easterly-winds prejudice your choicest Tulips, and spot them ; therefore cover such with Mats or Canvass to prevent freckles, and sometimes destruction. The same care have of your most precious Anemonies, Auricula's, Chamae-iris, Brumal Jacynths, Early Cyclamen, etc. Wrap your shorn Cypress Tops with Straw wisps, if the Eastern blasts prove very tedious. About the end uncover some Plants, but with Caution ; for the tail of the Frosts yet continuing, and sharp winds, with the sudden darting heat of the Sun, scorch and destroy them in a moment ; and in such weather neither sow nor transplant.

Sow Stock-gilly-flower seeds in the Fall to produce double flowers.

Now may you set your Oranges, Lemons, Myrtils, Oleanders, Lentises, Dates, Aloes, Amonumus, and like tender trees and Plants in the Portico, or with the windows and doors of the Green-houses and Conservatories open for eight or ten days before April, or earlier, if the Season invite, to acquaint them gradually with the Air ; but trust not the Nights, unless the weather be thoroughly settled.

Lastly, bring in materials for the Birds in the Aviary to build their nests withal.

FLOWERS IN PRIME, OR YET LASTING.

Anemonies, Spring Cyclamen, Winter Aconite, Crocus, Bellis, white and black Hellebor, single and double Hepatica, Leucoion, Chamae-iris of all colours, Dens Caninus, Violets, Fritillaria, Chelidonium, small with double Flower, Hermodactyls, Tuberous Iris, Hyacinth, Zenboin, Brumal, Oriental, etc. Junquils, great

117

Chalic'd, Dutch Mezereon, Persian Iris, Curialas, Narcissus with large tufts, common, double, and single, Prime Roses, Praecoce Tulips, Spanish Trumpets or Junquilles ; Violets, yellow Dutch Violets, Crown Imperial, Grape Flowers, Almonds and Peach-blossoms, Rubus odoratus, Arbour Judae, etc.

APRIL.

To be done

In the Orchard, and Olitory Garden.

Sow Sweet Marjoram, Hyssop, Basile, Thyme, Winter-Savoury, Scurvey-grass, and all fine and tender Seeds that require the Hot-bed.

Sow also Lettuce, Purslan, Cauly-flower, Radish, etc.
Plant Artichoke-slips, etc.
Set French-beans, etc.
You may yet slip Lavender, Thyme, Rose-mary, etc.
Towards the middle of this moneth begin to plant forth your Melons and Cucumbers, and to the late end ; your Ridges well prepared.

Gather up Worms and Snails, after evening showers, continue this also after all Summer rains.

Open now your Bee-hives, for now they hatch ; look carefully to them, and prepare your Hives, etc.

Fruits in Prime, and Yet Lasting.

APPLES.

Pepins, Deuxans, West-berry Apples, Russeting, Gilly-flowers, flat Reinet, etc.

PEARS.

Late Bon-crestien, Oak-pear, etc., double Blossom, etc.

119

APRIL.

To be done

In the Parterre, and Flower Garden.

Sow divers Annuals to have Flowers all the Summer ; as double Mari-golds, Cyanus of all sorts, Candy-tufts, Garden-Pansy, Muscipula, Scabious, etc.

Continue new, and fresh Hot-beds to entertain such exotic plants as arrive not to their perfection without them, till the Air and common earth be qualified with sufficient warmth to preserve them abroad. A Catalogue of these you have in the former Moneth.

Transplant such Fibrous roots as you had not finished in March ; as Violets, Hepatica, Prim-roses, Hellebor, Matricaria, etc.

Sow Pinks, Carnations, Sweet-Williams, etc., to flower next year ; this after rain.

Set Lupines, etc.

Sow also yet Pine-kernels, Firr-seeds, Phillyrea, Alaternus, and most perennial greens.

Now take out your Indian Tuberoses, parting the offsets (but with care, lest you break their fangs), then pot them in natural (not forc'd) Earth ; a layer of rich mould beneath, and about this natural earth to nourish the fibers, but not so as to touch the Bulbs ; then plunge your pots in a Hot-bed temperately warm, and give them no water till they spring, and then set them under a South-wall. In dry weather water them freely, and expect an incomparable flower in August. Thus likewise treat the Narcissus of Japan, or Garnsey-Lilly, for a late flower, and make much of this precious Direction.

Water Anemonies, Ranunculus's, and Plants in Pots and Cases once in two or three days, if drouth require it. But carefully protect from violent Storms of Rain and

KALENDARIUM HORTENSE

Hail, and the too parching darts of the Sun, your Pennach'd Tulips, Ranunculus's, Anemonies, Auricula's, covering them with Mattresses supported on cradles of hoops, which have now in readiness.

Now is the season for you to bring the choice and tender shrubs, etc., out of the Conservatory ; such as you durst not adventure forth in March. Let it be in a fair day ; only your Orange-trees may remain in the house till May, to prevent all danger.

Now, towards the end of April, you may Transplant and Remove your tender shrubs, etc., as Spanish Jasmines, Myrtils, Oleanders, young Oranges, Cyclamen, Pomegranats, etc., but first let them begin to sprout ; placing them a fort-night in the shade ; but about London it may be better to defer this work till August, vide also May. Prune now your Spanish Jasmine within an inch or two of the stock ; but first see it begin to shoot. Mow Carpet-walks, and ply Weeding, etc.

Towards the end (if the cold winds are past) and especially after showers, clip Philyrea, Alaternus, Cypress, Box, Myrtils, Barba Jovis, and other tonsile shrubs, etc.

FLOWERS IN PRIME, OR YET LASTING.

Anemonies, Ranunculus's, Auriculalirri, Chamae-Iris, Crown Imperial, Caprisolium, Cyclamen, Dens Caninus, Fritillaria, double Hepaticas, Jacynth starry, double Daisies, Florence-Iris, tufted Narcissus, white, double and common, English Double, Prime-rose, Cow-slips, Pulsatilla, Ladies-Smock, Tulips Medias, Ranunculus's of Tripoly, white Violets, Musk, Grape-flower, Parietaria Lutea, Leucoium, Lillies, Paeonies, double Jonquils, Muscaria revers'd, Cochlearia, Periclymenum, Aicanthus, Lilac, Rose-mary, Cherries, Wall-pears, Almonds, Abricots, White-Thorn, Arbour Judae blossoming, etc.

MAY.

To be done

In the Orchard, and Olitory Garden.

Sow Sweet-Marjoram, Basil, Thyme, hot and Aromatic Herbs, and Plants which are the most tender.

Sow Parslan, to have young; Lettuce, large-sided Cabbage, painted Beans, etc.

Look carefully to your Mellons; and towards the end of this moneth, forbear to cover them any longer on the Ridges, either with straw or mattresses, etc.

Ply the Laboratory, and distill Plants for Waters, Spirits, etc.

Continue Weeding before they run to Seeds.

Now set your Bees at full Liberty, look out often, and expect Swarms, etc.

Fruits in Prime, or Yet Lasting.

Pepins, Deuxans or John-Apples, West-berry-apples, Russeting, Gilly-flower Apples, the Maligan, etc., Codling.

PEARS.

Great Kainville, Winter-Bon-cretienne, Double Blossom-pear, etc.

CHERRIES, ETC.

The May-Cherry, Straw-berries, etc.

122

KALENDARIUM HORTENSE

MAY.

To be done

IN THE PARTERRE, AND FLOWER GARDEN.

Now bring your Oranges, etc., boldly out of the Conservatory; 'tis your only Season to Transplant, and Remove them; let the Cases be fill'd with natural-earth (such as is taken the first half spit, from just under the Turf of the best Pasture ground), mixing it with one part of rotten Cow-dung, or very mellow Soil screen'd and prepar'd some time before; if this be too stiff, sift a little Lime discreetly with it. Then cutting the Roots a little, especially at bottom, set your Plant; but not too deep; rather let some of the Roots appear. Lastly, settle it with temperate water (not too much) having put some rubbish of Brick-bats, Lime-stones, Shells, or the like at the bottom of the Cases, to make the moisture passage, and keep the earth loose. Then set them in the shade for a fort-night, and afterwards expose them to the Sun.

Give now also all your hous'd-plants fresh earth at the surface, in place of some of the old earth (a hand-depth or so) and loos'ning the rest with a fork without wounding the Roots. Let this be of excellent rich soil, such as is thoroughly consumed and with sift, that it may wash in the vertue, and comfort the Plant. Brush, and cleanse them likewise from the dust contracted during their Enclosure. These two last directions have till now been kept as considerable secrets amongst our gard'ners; vide August and September.

Shade your Carnations and Gilly-flowers after mid-day about this season. Plant also your Stock Gilly-flowers in beds, full Moon.

Gather what Anemony-seed you find ripe, and that is worth saving, preserving it very dry.

123

THE CHARM OF GARDENS

Cut likewise the stalks of such Bulbous-flowers as you find dry.

Towards the end, take up those Tulips which are dried in the stalk ; covering what you find to be bare from the Sun and showers.

FLOWERS IN PRIME, OR YET LASTING.

Late set Anemonies and Ranunculus nom. gen. Anapodophylon, Chamae-iris, Angustifol, Cyanus, Col-umbines, Caltha Palustris, double Cotyledon, Digitalis, Fraxinella, Gladiolus, Geranium, Horminum Creticum, yellow Hemerocallis, strip'd Jacynth, early Bulbous Iris, Asphodel, Yellow Lilies, Lychnis, Jacca, Bellis double, white and red, Millefolium Liteum, Lilium Con-valium, Span. Pinkes, Deptford-pinke, Rosa common, Cinnamon, Guelder and Centifol, etc. Syringa's, Sedunis, Tulips, Serotin, etc. Valerian, Veronica double and single, Musk Violets, Ladies Slipper, Stock-gilly-flowers, Spanish Nut, Star-flower, Chalcedons, ordinary Crow-foot, red Martagon, Bee-flowers, Campanula's white and bleu, Persian Lilly, Honey-suckles, Buglosse, Homers Moly, and the white of Dioscorides, Pansys, Prunella, purple Thalictrum, Sisymbrium, double and single, Leucoium bulbosum serstinum, Rose - mary Stacchas, Barba Jovis, Laurus, Satyrion, Oxyacanthus, Tamariscus, Apple-blossoms, etc.

JUNE.

To be done

IN THE ORCHARD, AND OLITORY GARDEN.

Sow Lettuce, Chevril, Radish, etc., to have young and tender Salleting.

About the midst of June you may inoculate Peaches, Abricots, Cherries, Plums, Apples, Pears, etc.

You may now also (or before) cleanse Vines of exuberant branches and tendrils, cropping (not cutting) and stopping the joynt immediately before the Blossoms, and some of the under branches which bear no fruit; especially in young Vineyards when they first begin to bear, and thence forwards.

Gather Herbs in the Fall, to keep dry; they keep and retain their virtue, and smell sweet, better dry'd in the shade than in the Sun, whatever some pretend.

Now is your season to distill Aromatic Plants, etc.

Water lately planted Trees, and put moist and half-rotten Fearn, etc., about the pot of their Stems.

Look to your Bees for Swarms, and Casts; and begin to destroy Insects with Hooses, Canes, and tempting baits, etc. Gather Snails after rain, etc.

FRUITS IN PRIME, OR YET LASTING.

APPLES.

Juniting (first ripe), Pepins, John-apples, Robillard, Red-Fennouil, etc., French.

THE CHARM OF GARDENS

The Maudlin (first ripe), Madera, Green-Royal, St. Laurence Pear, etc.

Black.

Duke, Flanders, Heart   Red.

White.

Luke-ward, early Flanders, the Common - cherry, Spanish - black, Naples - Cherries, etc. Rasberries, Corinths, Straw-berries, Melons, etc.

JUNE.

To be done

IN THE PARTERRE, AND FLOWER GARDEN.

Transplant Autumnal Cyclamens now if you would change their place, otherwise let them stand.

Gather ripe seeds of Flowers worth the saving, as of choicest Oriental Jacynth, Narcissus (the two lesser, pale spurious Daffodels of a whitish green often produce varieties), Auriculas, Ranunculus's, etc., and preserve them dry. Shade your Carnations from the afternoons Sun. Take up your rarest Anemonies, and Ranunculus's alter rain (if it come seasonable) the stalk wither'd, and dry the roots well. This about the end of the moneth. In mid June inoculate Jasmine, Roses, and some other rare shrubs. Sow now also some Anemony seeds. Take up your Tulip-bulbs, burying such immediately as you find naked upon your beds ; or else plant them in some cooler place ; and refresh over parched beds with water. Plant your Narcissus of Japan (that rare flower) in Pots, etc.

126

KALENDARIUM HORTENSE

Also you may now take up all such Plants and Flower-roots as endure not well out of the ground, and replant them again immediately : such as the Early Cyclamen, Jacynth Oriental, and other bulbous Jacynths, Iris, Fritillaria, Crown-Imperial, Martagon, Muscario, Dens Caninus, etc. The slips of Myrtil set in some cool and moist place do now frequently take root. Also Cytisus lunatus will be multiplied by slips, such as are an handful long that Spring. Look now to your Aviary ; for now the Birds grow sick of their feathers ; therefore assist them with Emulsions of the cooler seeds bruised water, as Melons, Cucumbers, etc. Also give them Succory, Beets, Groundsel, Chickweed, etc.

FLOWERS IN PRIME, OR YET LASTING.

Amaranthus, Antirrhinum, Campanula, Clematis Pannonica, Cyanus, Digitalis, Geranium, Horminum Creticum, Hieracium, bulbous Iris, and divers others, Lychnis, var. generum, Martagon white and red, Mille-folium, white and yellow, Nasturtium Indicum, Carnations, Pinks, Ornithogalum, Pansy, Phalangium Virginianum, darks-heel early. Pilosella, Roses, Thalaspi Creticum, etc. Veronica, Viola pentaphyl, Campions or Sultans, Mountain Lilies white and red ; double Poppies, Stock - jelly flowers, Jasmines, Corn - flag, Hollyhoc, Muscaria, serpyllum Citratum, Phalangium Allobrogicum, Oranges, Rose-mary, Leuticus, Pome-Granade, the Lime-tree, etc.

JULY.

To be done

IN THE ORCHARD, AND OLITORY GARDEN.

Sow Lettuce, Radish, etc., to have tender salleting.
Sow later Pease to be ripe six weeks after Michaelmas.

Water young planted Trees, and Layers, etc., and prune now Abricots, and Peaches, saving as many of the young likeliest shoots as are well placed ; for the new Bearers commonly perish, the new ones succeeding : Cut close and even.

Let such Olitory-herbs run to seed as you would save.

Towards the later end, visit your Vineyards again, etc., and stop the exuberant shoots at the second joint above the fruit ; but not so as to expose it to the Sun.

Now begin to straighten the entrance of your Bees a little ; and help them to kill their Drones if you observe too many ; setting Glasses of Beer mingled with Hony to entice the Wasps, Flyes, etc., which waste your store : also hang Bottles of the same Mixture near your Red-Roman Nectarines, and other tempting fruits for their destruction ; else they many times invade your best Fruit.

Look now also diligently under the leaves of Mural-Trees for the Snails ; they stick commonly somewhat above the fruit : pull not off what is bitten ; for then they will certainly begin afresh.

128

Beatrice Parsons

17. DAFFODILS IN A MIDDLESEX GARDEN

18. AN ORCHARD IN KENT

George S. Elgood, R.I.

19. A KENTISH GARDEN IN AUTUMN

B.E.Parsons

Beatrice Parsons

20. A HAMPSTEAD GARDEN IN WINTER

George S. Elgood, R.I.

21. A HERBACEOUS BORDER

Beatrice Parsons

22. BUSH AND RAMBLER ROSES

George S. Elgood, R.I.

23. THE SEAT BENEATH THE OAK

Beatrice Parsons

24. THE ROSE GARDEN, DRAKELOWE

Beatrice Parsons

25. THE GLORY OF EARLY SUMMER

Beatrice Parsons

26. A ROSE GARDEN

George S. Elgood, R.I.

27. THE GARDEN THAT I LOVE

Beatrice Parsons

28. A DOVECOT IN A SUSSEX GARDEN

29. LARKSPUR AND MEADOW-RUE

George S. Elgood, R.I.

30. A PATH IN A ROSE GARDEN

Helen Allingham, R.W.S.

31. A STANDARD ROSE BUSH

A. Heaton Cooper

32. AUTUMN COLOURS AT BONCHURCH OLD CHURCH,
NEAR VENTNOR, I.O.W.

KALENDARIUM HORTENSE

Fruits in Prime, or Yet Lasting.

APPLES.

Deuxans, Pepins, Winter-Russeting, Andrew-apples, Cinnamon-apple, red and white Juiniting, the Margaret-apple, etc.

PEARS

The Primat, Russet-pears, Summer-pears, green Chesil-pears, Pearl-pear, etc.

CHERRIES.

Carnations, Morella, Great-bearer, Morocco-cherry, the Egriot, Bigarreaux, etc.

PEACHES.

Nutmeg, Isabella, Persian, Newington, Violet-muscat, Rambouillet.

PLUMS, ETC.

Primordial, Myrobalan, the red, bleu, and amber Violet, Damax, Deuny Damax, Pear-plum, Damax, Violet or Cheson-plum, Abricot-plum, Cinnamon-plum, the Kings-plum, Spanish, Morocco-plum, Lady Eliz. Plum, Tawny, Damascene, etc.

Rasberries, Goose-berries, Corinths, Straw-berries, Melons, etc.

JULY.

To be done

In the Paterre, and Flower Garden

Slip Stocks and other lignous Plants and Flowers : From henceforth to Michaelmas you may also lay Gilly-

129

flowers and Carnations for Increase, leaving not above two, or three spindles for flowers, with supports, cradles, and hooses, to establish them against winds, and destroy Earwigs.

The Layers will (in a moneth or six weeks) strike root, being planted in a light loamy earth mix'd with excellent rotten soil and seifted : plant six or eight in a pot to save room in Winter : keep them well from too much Rains : but shade those which blow from the afternoons Sun, as in the former Moneths.

Yet also you may lay Myrtils, and other curious Greens.

Water young planted Shrubs and Layers, etc., as Orange-trees, Myrtils, Granades, Amomum, etc.

Clip Box, etc., in Parterres, knots, and Compartiments, if need be, and that it grow out of order ; do it after Rain.

Graff by Approach, Trench, or Innoculate Jasmines, Oranges, and your other choicest shrubs. Take up your early autumnal Cyclamen, Tulips and Bulbs (if you will Remove them, etc.) before mention'd ; Transplanting them immediately, or a Moneth after if you please, and then cutting off, and trimming the fibres, spread them to Air in some dry place.

Gather now also your early Cyclamen-seeds, and sow it presently in Pots.

Likewise you may now take up some Anemonies, Ranunculus's, Crocus, Crown Imperial, Persian Iris, Fritillaria, and Colchicums, but plant the three last as soon as you have taken them up, as you did the Cyclamens.

Remove now your Dens Canivus, etc.

Latter end of July seift your Beds for Off-sets of Tulips, and all Bulbous-roots, also for Anemonies—Ranunculus's, etc., which will prepare it for replanting with

130

such things as you have ready in pots to plunge, or
set in naked earth till the next season ; as Amaranths,
Canna Ind., Mirabile Peruv., Capsicum Ind., Nasturt.
Ind., etc., that they may not be empty and disfurnished.

Continue to cut off the wither'd stalks of your lower
flowers, etc., and all others, covering with earth the
bared roots, etc.

Now (in the driest season) with Brine, Pot-ashes,
and water, or a decoction of Tobacco refuse, water your
gravel-walks, etc., to destroy both worms and weeds, of
which it will cure them for some years.

Flowers in Prime, or Yet Lasting.

Amanauthus, Campanula, Clematis, Sultana, Veronica
purple and odoriferous ; Digitalis, Eryugium, Planum,
Ind. Phaseolus, Geranium triste, and Creticum, Lychnis
Chalcaedon Jacea white and double, Nasturt. Ind. Multe-
folium, Musk-rose, Flos Africanus, Thlaspi Creticum, etc.
Veronica mag. and parva, Volubilis, Balsam-apple, Holly-
hock, Snapdragon, Cornflo, Alkekengi, Lupius, Scorpion-
grass, Caryophlata om. gen. Stock-gilly-flo, Indian
Tuberous Jacynth, Limonium, Linaria Cretica, Pansies,
Prunella, Delphinium, Phalangium, Perploca Virgin,
Flos Passionis, Flos Cardinalis, Oranges, Amomum
Plinii, Oleanders red and white, Agnus Castus, Arbutus,
Yucca, Olive, Lignateum, Tilia, etc.

AUGUST.

To be done

IN THE ORCHARD, AND OLITORY GARDEN.

Inoculate now early, if before you began not.

Prune off yet also superfluous Branches, and shoots of this second spring; but be careful not to expose the fruit, without leaves sufficient to skreen it from the Sun, furnishing, and nailing up what you will spare to cover the defects of your Walls. Pull up the suckers.

Sow Raddish, tender Cabages, Cauly-flowers for Winter Plants, Corn-sallet, Marygolds, Lettuce, Carrots, Parnseps, Turneps, Spinage, Onions; also curl'd Endive, Angelica, Scurvy-grass, etc. Likewise now pull up ripe Onions and Garlic, etc.

Towards the end sow Purslan, Chard-Beet, Chervile, etc.

Transplant such Letuce as you will have abide all Winter.

Gather your Olitory-Seeds, and clip and cut all such Herbs and Plants within a handful of the ground before the fall. Lastley:

Unbind and release the buds you inoculated if taken, etc.

Now vindemiate and take your Bees towards the expiration of this Moneth; unless you see cause (by reason of the Weather and Season) to defer it till mid-September: But if your Stocks be very light and weak begin the earlier.

Make your Summer Perry and Cider.

KALENDARIUM HORTENSE

APPLES.

The Ladies Longing, the Kirkham Apple, John Apple ; the Seaming Apple, Cushion Apple, Spicing, May-flower, Sheeps-snout.

PEARS.

Windsor, Soveraign, Orange, Bergamot, Slipper Pearl, Red Catherine, King Catherine, Denny Pear, Prussia Pear, Summer Poppering, Sugar Pear, Lording Pea, etc.

PEACHES.

Roman Peach, Man Peach, Quince Peach, Rambouillet, Musk Peach, Grand Carnation, Portugal Peach, Crown Peach, Bourdeaux Peach, Lavar Peach, the Peach de-lepot, Savoy Malacoton, which lasts till Michaemas, etc.

NECTARINES.

The Muroy Nectarine, Tawny, Red-Roman, little Green Nectarine, Chester Nectarine, Yellow Nectarine.

PLUMS.

Imperial, Bleu, White Dates, Yellow Pear-plum, Black Pear-plum, White Nut-meg, late Pear-plum. Great Anthony, Turkey Plum, the Jane Plum.

OTHER FRUIT.

Cluster Grape, Muscadine, Corinths, Cornelians, Mulberries, Figs, Filberts, Melons, etc.

133

AUGUST.

To be done

IN THE PARTERRE, AND FLOWER GARDEN.

Now (and not till now if you expect success) is the just Season for the budding of the Orange Tree : Inoculate therefore at the commencement of this Moneth.

Now likewise take up your bulbous Iris's ; or you may sow their seeds, as also those of Larks-heel, Canditufts, Iron-colour'd Fox-gloves, Holly-hocks, and such plants as Endive Winter, and the approaching Seasons.

Plant some Anemony roots to have flowers all Winter, if the roots escape.

You may now sow Narcissus, and Oriental Jacynths, and replant such as will not do well out of the Earth, as Fritillaria, Iris, Hyacinths, Martagon, Dens Canivus.

Gilly-flowers may yet be slipp'd.

Continue your taking of Bulbs, Lilies, etc., of which before.

Gather from day to day your Alaternus seed as it grows black and ripe, and spread it to sweat and dry before you put it up ; therefore move it sometimes with a broom that the seeds may not clog together.

Most other seeds may now likewise be gathered from Shrubs, which you find ripe.

About mid-Aug. transplant Auricula's, dividing old and lusty roots ; also prick out your Seedlings : They best like a loamy sand or light moist Earth.

Now you may sow Anemony seeds, Ranunculus's, etc., lightly covered with fit mould in Cases, shaded, and frequently refresh'd : Also Cyclamen, Jacynths, Iris, Hepatica, Primroses, Fritillaria, Martagon, Fraxinella, Tulips, etc., but with patience ; for some of them because they flower not till three, four, five, six or seven

134

years after, especially the Tulips, therefore disturb
not their beds, and let them be under some warm place
shaded yet, till the heats are past, lest the seeds dry ;
only the Hepaticas, and Primeroses may be sow'd in
some less expos'd Beds.

Now, about Bartholomew-tide, is the only secure
season for removing and laying your perenial Greens,
Oranges, Lemmons, Myrtils, Phillyreas, Oleanders,
Jasmines, Arbutus, and other rare Shrubs, as Pome-
granads, Roses, and whatever is most obnoxious to
frosts, taking the shoots and branches of the past Spring
and pegging them down in a very rich earth and soil
perfectly consum'd, water them upon all occasions
during the Summer ; and by this time twelve-moneth
they will be ready to remove, Transplanted in fit earth,
set in the shade, and kept moderately moist, not over
wet, lest the young fibers rot ; after three weeks set
them in some more airy place, but not in the Sun till
fifteen days more ; vide our Observation in April, and
May, for the rest of these choice Directions.

FLOWERS IN PRIME, OR YET LASTING.

Amaranthus, Anagallis Lusitanica, Aster Atticus,
Blattaria, Spanish Bells, Bellevedere, Campanula,
Clematis, Cyclamen Vernum, Datura Turtica, Elio-
chryson, Eryngium planum, Amethystium, Geranium
Creticum and Triste, Yellow Stocks, Hieracion minus
Alpestre, Tube-rose Hyacinth, Limonium, Linaria
Cretica, Lychnis, Nimabile Peruvian, Yellow Mille-
foil, Nasturt : Ind. Yellow mountain Hearts-ease,
Manacoc, Africanus Flos, Convolvulus's, Scabious,
Asphodels, Lupines, Colchicum, Lencoion, Autumnal
Hyacinth, Holly-hoc, Star-wort, Heliotrop, French
Mary-gold, Daisies, Geranium nocte oleus, Common

135

THE CHARM OF GARDENS

Pansies, Larks-heels of all colours, Nigella, Lobello, Catch-fly, Thalaspi Creticum, Rosemary, Musk-rose, Monethly Rose, Oleanders, Spanish Jasmine, Yellow Indian Jasmine, Myrtils, Oranges, Pome-granads double and single flowers, Agnus Cactus, etc.

SEPTEMBER.

To be done

IN THE ORCHARD, AND OLITORY GARDEN.

Gather now (if ripe) your Winter Fruits, as Apples, Pears, Plums, etc., to prevent their falling by the great Winds : Also gather your Wind-falls from day to day ; do this work in dry weather.

Sow Lettuce, Radish, Spinage, Parsneps, Skirrets, etc. Cauly-flowers, Cabbage, Onions, etc. Scurvy-grass, Anis-seeds, etc.

Now you may Transplant most sorts of Esculent, or Physical plants, etc.

Also Artichocks, and Asparagus-roots.

Sow also Winter Herbs and Roots, and plant Strawberries out of the Woods.

Towards the end, earth up your Winter plants and Sallad herbs ; and plant forth your Cauly-flowers and Cabbages which were sown in August.

No longer now defer the taking of your Bees, streightening the entrances of such Hives as you leave to a small passage, and continue still your hostility against Wasps, and other robbing Insects.

Cider-making continues.

FRUITS IN PRIME, OR YET LASTING.

APPLES.

The Belle-bonne, the William, Summer Pearmain, Lordling-apple, Pear-apple, Quince-apple, Red-

137

greening ribbed, Bloody-Pepin, Harvey, Violet apple, etc.

PEARS.

Hamdens, Bergamot (first ripe), Summer Bon-crestien, Norwich, Black Worcester (baking), Green-field, Orange, Bergamot, the Queen hedge-pear, Lewes-pear (to dry excellent), Frith-pear, Arundel-pear (also to bake), Brunswick-pear, Winter Poppering, Bings-pear, Bishops-pear (baking), Diego, Emperours-pear, Cluster-pear, Messire Jean, Rowling-pear, Balsam-pear, Bezy d' Hery, etc.

PEACHES, ETC.

Malacoton, and some others, if the year prove backwards, almonds, etc.

Quinces.

Little Bleu-grape, Muscadine-grape, Frontiniac, Parsley, great Bleu-grape, the Verjuyce-grape, excellent for sauce, etc.

Bexberries, etc.

SEPTEMBER.

To be done

IN THE PARTERRE, AND FLOWER GARDEN.

Plant some of all the sorts of Anemonies after the first rains, if you will have flowers very forwards ; but it is surer to attend till October, or the Moneth after, lest the over moisture of the Autumnal seasons give you cause to repent.

Begin now also to plant some Tulips, unless you will stay until the later end of October, to prevent all hazard of rotting the Bulbs.

All Fibrous Plants, such as Hepatica, Hellebor,

Cammomile, etc. Also the Capillaries; Matricaria,
Violets, Prim-roses, etc., may now be transplanted.

Now you may also continue to grow Alaternus,
Philyrea (or you may forbear till the Spring), Iris, Crown
Imper; Martagon, Tulips, Delphinium, Nigella, Cand-
tufts, Poppy; and generally all the Annuals which are
not impair'd by the Frosts.

Your Tuberoses will not endure the wet of this Season;
therefore set the Pots into your Conserve, and keep
them very dry.

Bind up now your Autumnal Flowers, and Plants to
stakes, to prevent sudden gusts which will else prostrate
all you have so industriously rais'd.

About Michaelmas (sooner, or later, as the Season
directs) the weather fair, and by no means foggy, retire
your choice Greens, and rarest Plants (being dry) as
Oranges, Lemmons, Indian and Span. Jasmine, Oleanders,
Barba-Jovis, Amomum Plin. Citysus Lunatus, Cham-
alaca tricoccos, Cistus Ledon Clussii, Dates, Aloes,
Seduns, etc., into your Conservatory; ordering them
with fresh mould, as you were taught in May, viz.
taking away some of the utmost exhausted earth, and
stirring up the rest, fill the Cases with rich, and well
consumed soil, to wash in, and nourish the roots during
Winter; but as yet leaving the doors and windows
open, and giving them much Air, so the Winds be not
sharp, nor weather foggy; do thus till the cold being
more intense advertise you to enclose them altogether:
Myrtils will endure abroad neer a Moneth longer.

The cold now advancing, set such plants as will not
endure the House into the earth; the pots two or three
inches lower than the surface of some bed under a
Southern exposure: then cover them with glasses,
having cloath'd them first with sweet and dry Moss;
but upon all warm, and benigne emissions of the Sun

and sweet showers, giving them air, by taking off all
that covers them : Thus you shall preserve all your
costly and precious Marum Syriacum, Cistus's, Geranium
nocte olens, Flos Cardinalis, Maracoco, seedling Arbutus's (a very hardy plant when greater), choicest Ranunculus's, and Anemonies, Acacia Aegypt, etc. Thus
governing them till April.

Secrets not till now divulg'd.

Note that Cats will eat, and destroy your Marum
Syriac, if they can come at it.

Flowers in Prime, or Yet Lasting.

Amaranthus tricolor, and others ; Anagallis of Por-
tugal, Antirrhinum, African flo. Amomum, Plinii,
Aster Atticus, Belvedere, Bellies, Campanula's, Colchi-
cum, Autumnal Cyclamen, Chrysanthemum angustifol,
Eupatorium of Canada, Sun-flower, Stock-gill-flo.
Geranium Creticum and nocte olens, Gentianella
annual, Hieracion minus Alpestre, Tuberous Indian
Jacynth, Linaria Cretica, Lychnis Constant. single and
double ; Limonium, Indian Lilly Narciss. Pomum
Aureum, and Amoris, etc., Spinosum Ind. Marvel of
Peru, Mille-folium, yellow, Nasturtium Indicum, Per-
sian Autumnal Narcissus, Virgianium Phalagium, Indian
Phaseolus, Scarlet Beans, Convolvulus divers. gen., Candy
Tufts, Veronica, purple Volubilis, Asphodil, Crocus,
Garnsey Lily, or Narcissus of Japan, Poppy of all
colours, single and double, Malva arborescens, Indian
Pinks, Aethiopic Apples, Capsicum Ind. Gilly-flowers,
Passion-flower, Dature double and single, Portugal
Ranunculus's, Spanish Jasmine, yellow Virginian Jas-
mine, Rhododendron, white and red, Oranges, Myrtils,
Muske Rose, and Monethly Rose, etc.

140

OCTOBER.

To be done

Trench Grounds for Orcharding, and the Kitchin-garden, to lye for a Winter mellowing.

Plant dry Trees (i) Fruit of all sorts, Standard, Mural or Shrubs, which lose their lease ; and that so soon as it falls : But be sure you chuse no Trees for the Wall of above two years Graffing at the most.

Now is the time for Ablaqueation, and laying bare the Roots of old unthriving, or over hasty blooming trees.

Moon now decreasing, gather Winter-fruit that remains, weather dry ; take heed of bruising ; lay them up clean lest they Taint, Cut and prune Roses yearly.

Plant and Plash Quick-sets.

Sow all stony, and hard kernels and seeds, such as Cherry, Pear-plum, Peach, Almond-stones, etc. Also Nuts, Haws, Ashen, Sycomor and Maple keys ; Acorns, Beech-mast, Apple, Pear and Crab Kernel, for Stocks ; or you may defer it till the next Moneth towards the later end. You may yet sow Letuce.

Make Winter Cider, and Perry.

FRUITS IN PRIME, AND YET LASTING.

APPLES.

Belle-et-Bonne, William, Costard, Lordling, Parsley-apples Pearmain, Pear-apple, Honey-meal, Apis, etc.

141

PEARS.

The Caw-pear (baking), Green-butter-pear, Thorn-pear, Clove-pear, Roussel-pear, Lombart-pear, Russet-pear, Suffron-pear, and some of the former Moneth.

Bullis, and divers of the September Plums and Grapes, Pines, etc.

OCTOBER.

To be done

IN THE PARTERRE, AND FLOWER GARDEN.

Now your Hyacinthus Tuberose not enduring the wet, must be set into the house, and preserved very dry till April.

Continue sowing what you did in September, if you please : Also,

You may plant some Anemonies, and Ranunculus's, in fresh sandish earth, taken from under the turf ; but lay richer mould at the bottom of the bed, which the fibres may reach, but not to touch the main roots, which are to be covered with the natural earth two inches deep : and so soon as they appear, secure them with Mats, or Straw, from the winds and frosts, giving them air in all benigne intervals ; if possible once a day.

Plant also Ranunculus's of Tripoly, etc.

Plant now your choice Tulips, etc., which you feared to interre at the beginning of September ; they will be more secure and forward enough : but plant them in natural earth somewhat impoverish'd with very fine sand ; else they will soon lose their variegations ; some more rich earth may lye at the bottom, within reach of the fibres : Now have a care your Carnations catch not too much wet ; therefore retire them to covert, where they may be kept from the rain, not the air, Trimming them with fresh mould.

All sorts of Bulbous roots may now be safely buried ; likewise Iris's, etc.

You may yet sow Alaternus, and Phillyrea seeds ; it will now be good to Beat, Roll, and Mow Carpet-walks, and Camomile ; for now the ground is supple, and it will even all inequalities : Finish your last weeding, etc.

Sweep and cleanse your Walks, and all other places, of Autumnal leaves fallen, lest the worms draw them into their holes, and foul your Gardens, etc.

Flowers in Prime, or Yet Lasting.

Amaranthus tricolor, etc. Aster Atticus, Amomum, Antirrhinum, Colchicum, Heliotrope, Stock-gilly-flo., Geranium triste, Ind. Tuberose Jacynth, Limonium, Lychnis white and double, Pomum Amoris and Aethiop., Marvel of Peru, Millefol. luteum, Autumnal Narciss., Pansies, Aleppo Narciss., Sphaerical Narciss., Nasturt., Persicum, Gilly-flo., Virgin Phalangium, Pilosella, Violets, Veronica, Arbutus, Span. Jasmine Oranges.

NOVEMBER.

To be done

In the Orchard, and Olitory Garden.

Carry Comfort out of your Melon-ground, or turn and mingle it with the earth, and lay it in ridges ready for the Spring : Also trench and fit ground for Artichocks, etc.

Continue your Setting and Transplanting of Trees ; lose no time, hard frosts come on apace ; yet you may lay bare old Roots.

Plant young Trees, Standards or Mural.

Furnish your Nursery with Stocks to graff on the following year.

Sow and set early Beans and Pease till Shrove-tide ; and now lay up in your Cellars for Seed, to be Transplanted at Spring, Carrots, Parsneps, Turneps, Cabbages Cauly-flowers, etc.

Cut off the tops of Asparagus, and cover it with longdung, or make Beds to plant in Spring, etc.

Now, in a dry day, gather your last Orchard-fruits.

Take up your Potatoes for Winter spending, there will be enough remain for stock, though never so exactly gather'd.

Fruits in Prime, or Yet Lasting.

APPLES.

The Belle-bonne, the William, Summer Pearmain, Lordling-apple, Pear-apple, Cardinal, Winter Chess-

nut, Short-start, etc., and some others of the former two
last Moneths, etc.

PEARS.

Messire Jean, Lord-pear, long Bergamot, Warden
(to bake), Burnt Cat, Sugar-pear, Lady-pear, Ice-pear,
Dove-pear, Deadmans-pear, Winter Bergamot, Belle-
pear, etc.

Bullis, Medlars, Services.

NOVEMBER.

To be done

IN THE PARTERRE, AND FLOWER GARDEN.

Sow Auricula seeds thus : prepare very rich earth
more than half dung, upon that seift some very light
sandy mould ; and then sow ; set your Cases or Pans
in the Sun till March. Cover your peeping Ranunculus's, etc.

Now is your best season (the weather open) to plant
your fairest Tulips in place of shelter, and under Espaliers ; but let not your earth be too rich, vide Octob.
Transplant ordinary Jasmine, etc. About the middle
of this Moneth (or sooner, if weather require) quite
enclose your tender Plants, and perennial Greens,
Shrubs, etc., in your Conservatory, secluding all entrance of cold, and especially sharp winds ; and if the
Plants become exceeding dry, and that it do not actually
freeze, refresh them sparingly with qualified water
mingled with a little sheeps or Cow-dung : If the Season
prove exceeding piercing (which you may know by
the freezing of a dish of water set for that purpose in
your Green-house) kindle some Charcoal, and then
put them in a hole sunk a little into the floor about the

145

middle of it : This is the safest stove : at all other times when the air is warmed by the beams of a fine day, and that the Sun darts full upon the house shew them the light ; but enclose them again before the sun be gone off : Note that you must never give your Aloes, or Sedums one drop of water during the whole Winter.

Prepare also Mattresses, Boxes, Cases, Pots, etc., for shelter to your tender Plants and Seedlings newly sown, if the weather prove very bitter.

Plant Roses, Althæa Frutex, Lilac, Syringas, Cytisus, Peonies, etc.

Plant also Fibrous roots, specified in the precedent Moneth.

Sow also stony-seeds mentioned in Octob.

Plant all Forest-trees for Walks, Avenues, and Groves.

Sweep and cleanse your Garden-walks, and all other places, of Autumnal leaves.

FLOWERS IN PRIME, OR YET LASTING.

Anemonies, Meadow Saffron, Antirrhinum, Stock-gilly-flo., Bellis, Pansies, some Carnations, double Violets, Veronica, Spanish Jasmine, Musk Rose, etc.

DECEMBER.

To be done

In the Orchard, and Olitory Garden.

Prune, and Nail Wall-fruit, and Standard-trees.

You may now plant Vines, etc.

Also Stocks for Graffing, etc.

Sow, as yet, Pomace of Cider-pressings to raise Nurseries; and set all sorts of Kernels, Stones, etc.

Sow for early Beans, and Pease, but take heed of the Frosts; therefore surest to defer it till after Christmas, unless the Winter promise very moderate.

All this Moneth you may continue to Trench Ground and dung it, to be ready for Bordures, or the planting of Fruit-trees, etc.

Now seed your weak Stocks.

Turn and refresh your Autumnal Fruit, lest it taint and open the Windows where it lyes, in a clear and Serene day.

Fruits in Prime, or Yet Lasting.

APPLES.

Rousseting, Leather-coat, Winter-reed, Chest-nut Apple, Great-belly, the Go-no-further, or Cats-head, with some of the precedent Moneth.

PEARS.

The Squib-pear, Spindle-pear, Virgin, Gascoyne-Bergomot, Scarlet-pear, Stopple-pear, white, red, and French Wardens (to bake or roast), etc.

147

DECEMBER.

To be done

IN THE PARTERRE, AND FLOWER GARDEN.

As in January, continue your hostility against Vermine.

Preserve from too much Rain and Frost your choicest Anemonies, Ranunculus's, Carnations, etc.

Be careful now to keep the Doors and Windows of your Conservatories well matted, and guarded from the piercing Air : for your Oranges, etc., are now put to the test : Temper the cold with a few Char-coal govern'd as directed in November, etc.

Set Bay-berries, etc., dropping ripe.

Look to your Fountain-pipes, and cover them with fresh and warm litter out of the stable, a good thickness lest the frosts crack them ; remember it in time, and the Advice will save far both trouble and charge.

FLOWERS IN PRIME, OR YET LASTING.

Anemonies some, Persian, and Common Winter Cyclamen, Antirrhinum, Black Hellebor, Laurus tinus, single Prim-roses, Stock-gilly-flo., Iris Clusii, Snow-flowers, or drops, Yucca, etc.

PART IV

GARDEN MOODS

I

TOWN GARDENS:

Few people will deny the peace of mind a sheet of green grass can give, but few people, one imagines, trouble to think how they are preserved in large Towns and Cities. If it were not for Societies many little open spaces would years ago have been covered with streets of houses, many fair trees have fallen, none have been planted, and those growing have been neglected and allowed to die. Of the many Societies whose work has been to preserve for the Public pleasure grounds, good trees, parks, and flower gardens, not one deserves such praise as the Metropolitan Public Gardens Association, whose great work has been carried on since 1882.

When one considers that in Hampstead over six hundred acres have been preserved by energetic Committees from the hands of builders it is easy to see how great is the debt of London to those who voluntarily work for this and other Open Space Societies.

It is not, however, by these large tracts of open country that the towns and cities alone benefit. Seats, fountains, flower beds, and pavements have been placed in old church-yards and disused burial-grounds opened for the benefit of the public. One has only to look at the map of the Metropolitan Public Gardens Association to see how wonderful their work has been and still is,

151

THE CHARM OF GARDENS

To dwellers in Towns the sight of flowers in the streets is like a breath of the country. The long line of flower-sellers in the High Street, Kensington, one group of women in Piccadilly Circus, in Oxford Circus, in other spots where the place of their flower baskets brightens all the neighbourhood, are doctors, though they do not know it, of high degree. They bring the message of the changing year. They are a perpetual flower calendar, people to whom a reverence is due. One looks in Piccadilly Circus for the first Snowdrops, the little knots of their delicate white faces peering over the edge of the flower baskets. From the tops of omnibuses the first Violets are seen. Anemones have their turn, and Mimosa, and Cowslips, and Roses soon glow in the midst of the traffic, and elegant Carnations in their silver grass, and great piles of Asters. So we may read the year. All through the grey and desolate Winter these flower women hold their own, through cold and rain, and pale Winter sun they keep the day alive with the glowing colours of flowers. I often wonder, as I see them sit there so patiently, if they know the joy they give the passer-by, or if they are more like the rocks on whom flowers grow by nature. They are a curious race, these flower-women, untidy, with a screw of hair twisted up under a battered hat of black straw, with faded shawls wrapped round them, and the weapons of their craft arranged about them—jam jars of water, wire, bass, rows of little sticks on the end of which button-holes are stuck. And they have wonderful contrivances for keeping their money, ancient purses rusty like many of themselves, in which greasy pennies and wet sixpences wallow in litters of dirty paper. I would not vouch for the truth of all they say, for it would appear from their words that every flower in their baskets is but just picked, or only that second from the market.

152

And they regard such evidence as withered and wet flower stalks with half-humorous scorn. For all they may not be well favoured, and a pretty flower-woman is as rare as a dead donkey, still, for me, they have a certain dingy dignity, or rather a natural picturesque quality as of lichen on the pavements.

These people are the town's gardens of odd corners, while another tribe of them are perambulating gardens bringing sudden colour into the soberest of streets. There are those who carry enormous baskets on their heads, and cry in some incomprehensible tongue words intended to convey a message such as "All fresh." To see a gorgeous glowing mass of Daffodils sway down the street borne triumphantly aloft like the litter of some Princess is one of those sights to repay many grey days. Then the brothers to this tribe are those who carry from street to street Ferns and Lilies on carts, drawn often by a patient ass. I own feeling a distrust for these men, they do not dispense their goods with much love. They are not eloquent, as are many flower women in praise of the beauties of the India plant, or the Shuttle-cock Ferns. I feel that they are interlopers in the business, and have failed at the hardware trade, or have no capacity for the selling of rush baskets, or the grinding of scissors. At the heels of all those who sell flowers in the streets are the out-cast members of the tribe, men with brutal faces who follow lonely women in unfrequented streets trying to thrust dead plants upon them, and cursing if they are not bought. And there are the aged crones who sit by the railings of little squares and hold out a tray of boot laces, matches, a few very suspicious-looking Apples, and, in the corner, a bunch of dead flowers—a kind of æsthetic appeal.

Your true flower-lover will search as carefully among their baskets for the object of his desire as will the

153

collector the musty curiosity shops for prizes for his collection. There comes the time when the first Snow-drops, their stalks tied with wool, appear here and there and may be brought home as rare prizes. A word here of flower vases. Clear glass is the only form of vessel for any kind of flower. I feel certain of that. No crock, no form of pottery gives out greater the real value to your cut flowers. The stalks are part of the beauty of the flower, the submerged leaf as lovely as the leaf above. And, above and beyond all things, glass shows at once if your water is pure, and if your vase is full. Nowadays beautiful striped glass vases are made and sold so cheaply that there is no excuse for the old, and often ugly, pot vases so many people use. I own to a certain liking to seeing roses in old China bowls, but have a lurking suspicion that I am Philistine in this.

There is, of course, a distinction between Town Gardens and gardens in Towns. The one being the open free spaces dedicated to the pleasure of Duke and tramp alike : the other the hidden and hallowed spots where the town dweller fights soot, grime, smoke, and lack of sun, and fights them in many cases wonderfully well. One finds, though, that many people fancy that only Ivy, cats, and dustbins will flourish in the heart of a smoky City. This is not the case. Broom, Lilac, Trumpet Flower, Travel-ler's Joy, many kinds of Honeysuckle, Passion Flower, Tulip Tree, many kinds of Cherry and Plum Trees bear-ing beautiful blossoms, Barberry, and Almond Trees— all these will grow well and strongly even in the worst parts of London. Five kinds of Honeysuckle will flourish ; they are :

Lonicera	Lepebouri	Lonicera	Serotinum
„	Flexuosam	„	Belgicum
„	Brachypoda aurea		

154

Besides these, pink and white Brambles, Meadowsweet, Weigela, and Rhododendrons all grow fairly easily.

One of the first sights the traveller notices on approaching any large town is the numerous and gay back gardens of the little houses. The contents of these gardens are a true index to the inhabitants of the houses. Where one garden boasts little but old packing-cases, drying linen, a few stalks of hollyhocks, and one or two giant sunflowers, the very next will show borders full of all varieties of flowers in season, an eloquent picture of what may be done with a little trouble. The consolation and pleasure these little town gardens give is out of all proportion to their size. The man who can come home to a villa, however badly built and hideous, and it often appears that some competition in ugliness has won suburban prizes, can find a delight all good gardeners know in working his plot of land.

One thing we can see at a glance, that the good influence of one well-kept garden in a row will very soon have its effect. There is one street I know within the bounds of London, a street of new houses with little gardens in front of them running down to the pavement. I watched this street with interest from its very beginning. At first it was a thing of beauty, the men at work on the buildings, the scaffolding against the sky, the horses and carts waiting with loads of brick, the gradual growth of the houses from foundation to roof. Even the ugliest building is beautiful in the course of construction, the poles and ladders hiding the coarse design. Then there came a day when the street was finished. It is not an entire street, but about half, being a row of twenty or so houses built in flats, three flats in each house. When the men left and the houses stood naked, after the plan of the builder, looking pitiful and commonplace, the new red brick was raw, the little balconies very white and staring, the windows like blind eyes. Every ground-floor flat had the disadvantage of less light and air than the others, but it was the possessor of about nine feet of land between the door and the pavement. For a long time I waited to see what would become of this tenant-less row of houses. I gained a kind of affection for them, and walked past the white signboards once or twice a week reading always " To Let " written on the windows, painted on the notice board, pasted on papers across the doors. The melancholy aspect of these houses appealed to me ; they had a look of dumb anxiety as if they longed to hear the sound of voices in their empty rooms. At last I saw one day three huge furniture vans drawn up in front of the houses, and during the next two weeks more vans arrived and there was a sound of hammering in the street, and a smell of unpacking. Men came there with boxes and parcels, and tradesmen began to drive up in carts and motor-cars. I felt that those houses still standing empty had a jealous look in their windows, like little girls who had been left to sit out at a dance. The notice boards were all shifted to their front gardens, their bell wires still hung unconnected from holes by the front door.

The thing I was really waiting to see happened at Number Two. The builder, after finishing the houses had, I suppose, come to the conclusion that a little help from Nature would do no harm. Some good fairy prompted him to plant Almond and May Trees alternate-ly in the front gardens. To each house an Almond and a May. I had waited eagerly, determining by some fan-tastic twist that the spirit of the new houses would first make her appearance in one of these trees. So far the street had possessed no character except that vague rawness that all new places wear. The great event occurred at Number Two. Very delicately an Almond tree put out the first blossom. The life of the street began. I did not wonder about the favoured owners of the ground floor of Number Two. I knew.

Not long after the Almond tree had bloomed a cart drew up before Number Two, and three men began to wheel barrow loads of earth into the front garden. They were directed by a gentleman of some age, but of cheerful countenance. He smiled as each load of earth was neatly placed. He looked at the earth as if he already saw it covered with flowers. In his mind's eye he was arranging a surprise for the street.

The next event of notice in the street was the appearance of Number Two garden, a blaze of flowers set in a desert of red brick. A balcony of Number Sixteen, far down the road, entered into friendly competition. Numbers Five and Nine worked like slaves. Three followed suit with carpet-bedding on a tiny scale. A Laburnam and a Lilac sprang like magic from the soil of Number Ten. Then, one day, the whole of Number One burst into flower from top to toe. The tenant of each floor having apparently been secretly at work to surprise the rest. Two, who had started, and was indeed the father of the street, put forth more strenuous efforts.

To-day I am certain of a pleasant walk, and can come out of a wilderness of bricks and mortar to my charming oasis flowering in the land. I wonder if the people who live in those flats and who compete with each other in a friendly rivalry of blossom realise what they are doing for the hundreds who pass by in the day and are cheered.

The Association I have named before, the Metropolitan Public Gardens Association, give in their statement for 1907 a list of their window garden competitions for that year. One sees that many of the poorer parts of London have taken the idea, and this note I quote from South Hackney shows the result: " Twelve entries.

THE CHARM OF GARDENS

Eight prizes of the total amount of One Pound, **Ten** Shillings. Remarks : Clean, fresh-looking, more creepers than last year ; example set is improving character of roads, as others, not competitors, have started gardens."

Any one who knows the dreary and desolate appearance of town streets, especially in those parts where life is lived at the hardest, and surroundings are of the most sordid, will encourage a work which induced in one year over five hundred people in London slums to take an interest in growing flowers.

The *Spectator*, of September 6, 1712, contains a charming essay upon the English Garden, and the writer draws attention to Kensington Gardens in the following words :

" I shall take notice of that part in the upper gardens at Kensington, which was at first nothing but a Gravel Pit. It must have been a fine Genius for gardening, that could have thought of forming such an unsightly Hollow into so beautiful an Area, and to have hit the eye with so uncommon and agreeable a Scene as that which it is now wrought into. To give this peculiar spot of ground the greater effect, they have made a very pleasing contrast ; for as on one side of the Walk you see this hollow Bason, with its several little Plantations lying so conveniently under the Eye of the Beholder ; on the other side of it there appears a seeming Mound, made up of trees rising one higher than another in proportion as they approach the Centre. A Spectator who has not heard this account of it, would think this Circular Mount was not only a real one, but that it had been actually scooped out of that hollow space which I have before mentioned. I never yet met with anyone who has walked in this Garden, who was not struck with that Part of it which I have mentioned."

158

TOWN GARDENS

The writer finishes his essay with a simple and rather delightful passage :

" You must know, Sir, that I look upon the Pleasure which we take in a Garden, as one of the innocent Delights in human Life. A Garden was the Habitation of our first Parents before the Fall. It is naturally apt to fill the mind with Calmness and Tranquillity, and to lay all its turbulent Passions at rest. It gives us a great Insight into the Contrivance and Wisdom of Providence, and suggests innumerable subjects for Meditation. I cannot but think the very Complacency and Satisfaction which a man takes in these Works of Nature, to be a laudable, if not a virtuous Habit of Mind."

Our opinion has not altered in these two hundred years. The enjoyment of a garden is certainly one of the most innocent delights in human life, the enjoyment of the garden he mentions in particular is one of the most innocent pleasures in London. Kensington Gardens have inspired many people, the classic of them is undoubtedly Mr. J. M. Barrie's " Little White Bird." The patron Saint of them is, and I think ever will be, " Peter Pan." One has only to walk down the Babies Mile to hear games from Peter Pan going on in all directions. This peculiar spirit haunted the Gardens long before the days of Mr. Barrie, and whispered much of his charming story in the ears of a bewigged gentleman— Mr. Tickell, by name—who, in a poem of some considerable length, sang Kensington's praises. Those tiny fairy trumpets sounding in the walks of Kensington sounded a tune which has never left the air, and one fancies the creator of Peter Pan catching sight of a dim ghost now and again, the ghost of Mr. Tickell, Joseph Addison's friend, as he walks in full-bottomed

159

wig, his wide skirted coat, and sees the fairies too. He begins :

> Where Kensington high o'er the neighb'ring lands
> 'Midst greens and sweets, a regal fabric stands,
> And sees each spring, luxuriant in her bowers,
> A snow of blossoms, and a wild of flowers,
> The dames of Britain oft in crowds repair
> To groves and lawns, and unpolluted air.
> Here, while the town in damps and darkness lies,
> They breathe in sunshine, and see azure skies ;
> Each walk, with robes of various dyes bespread,
> Seems from afar a moving tulip-bed,
> Where rich biscades and glossy damasks glow,
> And chints, the rival of the show'ry bow.
>
> .   .   .   .   .
>
> Their midnight pranks the sprightly fairies play'd
> On every hill, and danced in every shade.
> But, foes to sunshine, most they took delight
> In dells and dales conceal'd from human sight :
> There hew'd their houses in the arching rock ;
> Or scoop'd the bosom of the blasted oak ;

There is no doubt about it that these are the very same fairies who are still at work in the Gardens, and who have admitted Mr. Barrie into their confidence. All gardens have ghosts, and Kensington Gardens, I think, more ghosts than any other. What a club it must be to belong to, to visit when all London is asleep. Here's Mr. Tickell with his version of the Peter Pan story :

> No mortal enter'd, those alone who came
> Stolen from the couch of some terrestrial dame
> For oft of babes they robb'd the matron's bed.

But beyond these, the vaguest hints, Mr. Tickell does not carry. His story has no likeness to the immortal tale of Peter Pan, but has, in common with it, the same knowledge that there are fairies in the Gardens living just as both he and Mr. Barrie know so well under the

160

roots of trees. And then there are the children. It is they who are the sweetest flowers of the town gardens.

If any man wants an argument in favour of keeping every available space open in towns and cities let him go into some crowded neighbourhood and watch the children playing in the gutters of the streets. Then let him find one of those places, a disused burial ground, or the garden of an old square, which has been preserved, and kept open, and laid out for the benefit of the children, and he will see the difference at once. There are two such places easy for the Londoner to visit, the one Browning Hall Garden, now a garden, once the York Road Burial Ground, Walworth, the other Meath Gardens, eleven acres of public garden, once The Victoria Park Cemetery, Bethnal Green.

They say that one half of London doesn't know how the other half lives. They do not know, but worse still they don't care. It is equally true that half the people who profess to care for flowers are ignorant of the wonderful flower-beds carefully grown for their pleasure within a two-penny 'bus ride of most parts of London. The row of beds facing Park Lane; the flower walk (where the babies walk, too) in Kensington Gardens ; the flower walk in Regent's Park, the Houses at Kew, are sights as well worth an afternoon's excursion as any other form of amusement. Most people almost unconsciously absorb the colour of cities, vaguely realising grey streets, red streets, white streets, spaces of grass and trees, big blots of colour—like the huge beds of scarlet geraniums in front of Buckingham Palace, but they do not trouble to get the value of their impressions. People look on the way from Hyde Park Corner to the Marble Arch as a convenient means of crossing London instead of one of the most interesting and delightful experiences to be had. They go crazy over trees and sky in the country, when

they have at their doors sights the country can never
equal.   The sun in late autumn setting behind the trees
of Hyde Park and glowing over the murky smoke-laden
skies is a sight for the gods.   Smoke has its disadvan-
tages, but it certainly gives one æsthetic joys unknown
in clear skies, for instance alone the reflection of the
lights of Piccadilly on the evening sky.

After all, the time to see the wonder of town gardens
is at night.   The streets are empty of people.   Here and
there a few night workers walk the lonely streets, a
policeman tramps his beat, the huge carts bringing the
provisions for the city lumber along with sleepy carters
swaddled in sacks perched high among the heaps of
baskets.   Here and there men with long hoses are washing down the roads.   The Parks and Gardens lie bathed
in peace, mysterious shadows make velvet caves sheltered
by leaves.   Those trees standing close to the road are lit
by the electric lamps and fringe the street with vivid
green.   Only the flowers seem really awake, alive, in a
tremendous dream city.   Along the lines of houses,
blinds down, shutters closed, a window box here and
there breaks the monotony and seems to be the only real
thing there.   If it is Spring, then from Hyde Park
Corner to the Kensington High Street, all along the side
of the Park, behind the railings are regiments of Crocus
flowers, spikes of Narcissus, and of Daffodil.   Their
sweetness fills the air, their very presence fills the town
with gentleness, and purifies and softens its grimness.
Far above, in some citadel of flats, a solitary light burns,
some one is at work, or ill, or watching.   Above all hang
the blazing stars.

II
THE EFFECT OF TREES

OF the pleasure and affect of trees no one speaks so
wisely as Bacon. Although those who have a feeling
for garden literature know his essay on Gardens as the
classic of its kind, still many do not recall his thoughts
when the planning of a garden is on hand.   Too much,
I think, is given by the man who is about to make a
garden, to his own particular hobby, and many a man
wonders why his garden gives him not all the pleasure
he expected.   You will hear of a man talk of his new
Rose beds, of the nursery for Carnations he is in the process of making, of the placing of his Violet frames, of
his ideas for a rock garden (I think the distressful feeling
for a rockery of clinkers is dead), but you will seldom
hear of a man who deliberates quietly for effects of
trees, or who thinks of planting fruit trees as ornaments,
but always he places them in his kitchen garden, and
ignores their value in their other proper places.

Bacon rejoices in his arrangement of gardens for every
month of the year, and dwells, rightly, just as much on
the pleasure of his trees as in the ordering of his flower
beds.   Naturally he had not such a large selection of
flowers from which to choose as we have to-day, but
to-day we neglect the beauty of many trees, and especially the beauty of hedges.

Are there sights in any garden more beautiful that
the Almond tree and the Peach tree in blossom, or the

163

sweet trailing Sweetbriar ? Bacon would have us notice these, make a feast of these. Also he recommends the beauty of the White Thorn in leaf, the Cherry and the Plum trees in blossom, the Cherry tree in fruit, the Lilac tree, the wonder of the Apple tree, and the Medlar.

Then, again, Bacon touches on a point all too little counted : the perfume of the garden. He says : " And because the breath of flowers is far sweeter in the air (where it comes and goes like the warbling of musick) than in the hand, therefore nothing is more fit for that delight than to know what be the flowers and plants that do best perfume the air.

" Roses, damask and red, are fast flowers of their smells ; so that you may walk by a whole row of them and find nothing of their sweetness ; yea, though it be in a morning's dew. Bays likewise yield no smell as they grow ; Rosemary little ; nor Sweet Marjorum.

" That which above all others yield the sweetest smell in the air is the Violet, especially the White Double Violet which comes twice a year ; about the middle of April, and about Bartholomew-tide. Next to that is the Musk Rose ; then the Strawberry leaves dying, which yield a most excellent cordial smell. Then the flowers of the Vines ; it is a little dust, like the dust of a Bent, which grows upon the cluster, in the first coming forth : then the Sweet Briar, then Wallflowers, which are very delightful to be set under a parlour or lower chamber window. Then Pinks and Gilly-flowers, especially the matted Pink and Clove Gilly-flower : then the flowers of the Lime tree ; then the Honeysuckles, so they be somewhat afar off.

" Of Bean flowers I speak not, because they are field flowers.

" But those which perfume the air most delightfully,

not passed by as the rest, but being trodden upon and crushed, are three, that is Burnet, Wild Thyme, and Water Mints. Therefore, you are to set whole alleys of them to have the pleasure when you walk or tread. I would add to these one or two more flowers whose perfume is easily yielded. The Heliotrope, which at night will scent a garden ; and Stocks, very rich and sweet scented ; Tobacco Plant, a heavy sensuous smell ; Madonna Lilies, seeming almost to breathe ; Evening Primroses ; and, after rain when the sun is warm, the leaves of Geraniums, a faint musky smell, very attractive. But of all these the garden holds one perfume more delicious, a scent that, to me at least, is the Queen of Garden scents since it is the breath of the whole garden herself. After a Summer's day when it has been hot and the lawn has been cut, and the Sun has well baked the earth, if there should come rain in the evening, a soft warm rain pattering at first so that it seems each leaf of flower and tree becomes a drum sounding with rain beats, then it seems the garden breathes deep and draws in great draughts of the delicious coolness. Then after the rain the night comes warm again, and all warm earth smells, and the new cut grass smells also, and every tree and flower join force upon force until the air is filled with a perfume which for want of better names I would call the Odour of Gratitude."

Furthermore, Bacon speaks of the garden—" The garden is best to be square, encompassed on all four sides with a stately arched hedge." One rich hedge is there at Bishopsbourne, which it is traditionally supposed was planted by Richard Hooker, of whom Walton writes : " It is a hedge of over one hundred feet in length, from twelve to fourteen feet in height, and some ten feet thick. It is one of the finest Yew hedges in England, a wonderful colour, an amazing strength and beautiful, when it is clipped and trimmed, to look upon." Of the pleasure and comfort of such hedges, of the health to be gained by regarding them, many people have spoken. There is, surely, something in the tough green life of the Yew, something in its staunchness that conveys a feeling of strength to the mind. I feel this in different degree with every kind of tree, partly no doubt from moments of particular association, from memories that become attached to scenes as they will (curious how scents, arrangements of colour, outlines against a sky, will call up things and thoughts which for the moment have no connection with them. I never see Oranges but I think of a dark passage lined with books, and a cupboard built round with books in shelves. In the cupboard are dishes of fruit, and shapes, all tied up in linen, of fruit cheeses, as damson cheese, and crab-apple cheese, and a cheese made of Quinces and Medlars).

I remember a graveyard in a little Swiss village where every grave had a tiny weeping willow bending over it. It had, for us, infinitely more pathos than the sombreness of many English graveyards. There was a rushing torrent below, for the church and its grave-yard was on a height over a river, and the voice of the river sang in the quiet graveyard, like a strong spirit singing in the pride of vigour to those asleep. The little willows bent and shivered in the breeze, looking small and pathetic against the strong small church. Outside the church, all along one wall was a seat very smooth and worn, it faced the graves and the tiny trees, and behind it, on the wall of the church, was a great Wisteria with clusters of pale purple flowers. There were no other trees there, or to be seen from the seat, but these little bending weeping trees. And close by, a hundred yards from the church gate, was the undertaker's shop, part farm, part garden, part stocked with elm planks. As I passed by the son was making a coffin out in the middle of the road on trestles. Looking back one could see the young man bending earnestly over his work, the sound of his saw ripping the air. Behind him was the grey stone of the church and the forest of little shivering trees over the graves. A little below, just across the river over a covered bridge, was a beer-garden where a family was sitting drinking beer out of tall mugs. They sat, father, mother, sons and daughters, all dressed in black, under Chestnut trees cut down very close and clipped to make alleys of shade. And a little behind them was a forest rising on a hill with great masses of trees all shades of green, and glowing in the light of an afternoon sun. But of all this I carry mostly the memory of those little trees, quiet weeping sentinels, very pathetic.

Trees, especially isolated groups of trees, in towns and cities have a wonderful fascination. The very idea that they burst into bud and leaf in the midst of all the smoke and grime, and the noise and hurry, is health-giving. It brings repose, it brings hope. I believe the trees in town squares get more love than any country trees. They mean so much. It seems so good of them to fight, and to come out year by year clean and fresh and green, and in Winter when they are bare they make a delicate webwork of twigs against the background of soot-covered houses. Then in the Spring when they turn faintly purple there is a haze across the square, and it seems that even the pigeons and the horses on the cab rank feel it, but cannot scarcely believe it. Then, perhaps there is an Almond tree in the square and it will suddenly break out into the most exquisite finery, like the daintiest of women, making the square gay and full of joy. The Spring has come. It is almost unbelievable. And people passing through the square who have forgotten all about the Spring look up suddenly and smile, and say : " Look at the Almond tree. Spring is here." Those who know the country turn their minds inwards and remember that the brown owls have begun to hoot, that the gossamer is floating, that, here and there yellow and white butterflies are flitting, looking strangely out of season, that the raven is building, and the rooks too, and that all sorts of birds they had forgotten are seen in the land.

After that the big trees in the square become hazy with bursting bud, and one morning, as if some message had been whispered overnight, the far side of the square is only to be seen through a screen of the tenderest green. Bit by bit the leaves comes out, get bright, clean washed by showers, get dingy with the soot. Then comes the fall of the leaf and the crisp curl of it as it changes colour, and the far side of the square begins to show again through bronze-coloured leaves. At last the Winter comes and all that is left is the tracery of boughs and twigs, and heaps of dead, beautiful-coloured leaves beneath the trees. These still provide an interest, for the wind comes and picks them up and whirls them right up into the air in all sorts of amazing dances and games.

In the Winter one last beauty comes. The day has been leaden, sad-coloured, bitterly cold. All the cabmen on the rank stamp with their feet, and swing their arms to keep themselves warm, and there is a little mist where all the horses breathe. And people coming through the square have forgotten the Almond tree, and the look of the big trees when the hot sun splashed gold on their leaves, and they say, looking at the sky, " See how dark it is, it is going to snow." The snow

comes ; the sky is darker ; the trees stick up looking
black, like drawings in pen and ink. Flakes, white
flakes, twenty, forty, then a rush—a thousand ; the sky
full of tiny white flakes, the air full of them whirling
down. All sounds begin to be muffled. Horses hoofs
beat with a thud on the ground. The sound of voices
in the air is deadened. The voices of men encouraging
horses sound sharp now and again, or a whip cracks
like a shot. The square is covered with snow, every
twig is outlined in white, black patches of bark show
here and there, and emphasise the dead whiteness.
When it has stopped snowing and a watery light comes
from the sun all the trees gleam wonderfully, looking
like fairy trees. And people passing through the
square making beaten tracks in the snow saying, " It
is Winter."

In a country garden there is a tree stands on the end
of a lawn. It is an Acacia tree, old, gnarled, and twisted,
with Ivy round it, deep Ivy in which thrushes build
year after year ; there is a stone near by on which the
thrushes break the shells of snails, the " tap, tap," of
the birds at work is one of the peaceful sounds that
break the silence of the garden.

Under the tree is an oblong mark of pressed grass
greener than the rest of the lawn, where the garden-
roller rests. And there is a seat under the tree, and a
wooden foot-rest by it.

Touch the tree and you go back at once to a picture
of a boy, the boy who helped to plant it over a hundred
and fifty years before. If you look from the tree across
the lawn to the house you will see the very door by
which he came out with his father to plant the tree.

The house and the tree have grown old together, both
of them have mellowed with the garden and wear a look

of old security and calm, and have an air of wise old age.

Up and down the five white steps from the garden path to the house more than five generations have passed, men in wide-skirted coats and full wigs hanging about their ears in great corkscrew curls, men in powdered wigs, rolled stockings, square buckled shoes, men in stocks and immense collars, and big frills to their shirts making them look like gentlemanly fish, down to the man who comes out to day who looks a little old-fashioned, and is square-built like the house, and who parts his hair like the men in Leech's pictures, and who wears a rim of whisker round his face. And troops of ladies have passed out by that door into the garden in hoops, and sacques, and towers of hair, and crinolines. But no lady comes out now to cut the Lavender hedge, or snip at the Roses. The man is alone. But when he sits alone under the tree, with a spud by his side ready to uproot Plantains from his lawn, he can see troops of the garden ghosts sitting round him under the Acacia tree.

Sometimes there seems to be a sound of the ghostly click of bowls on the lawn, for it is a bowling-green banked up on three sides (the fourth bank has been done away with long ago), and there is a company of gentlemen in their wide shirt sleeves playing bowls. Above them, on the raised terrace next to the house where there is a broad path, a group of old people sit by little tables and drink wine, and smoke, and gossip. And behind them are tall Hollyhocks, and Roses and a tangle of old-fashioned flowers such as Periwinkles and Sweet Williams, and Pinks. The Acacia tree, which grows on the lawn beyond the bowling green, is quite small.

The old man who dreams of these ghosts in his garden

recognises them readily because they have stepped out of pictures on his walls, and when they are not haunting the garden are demurely hanging on the oak panels in the old rooms.

Then he can see, if he chooses, a picture of the garden when the acacia tree is quite tall, but still elegant and slender, and in this picture an old, old lady walks down the garden paths. She is dressed in a large hooped skirt with panniers, and has high-heeled shoes, and a perfect tower of hair on her head, and over that a calash hood like the hood over a waggon except that it is black. She carries an ebony stick in a silk-mittened hand, a hand knotted with gout and covered with the mourning rings of her friends. She it was who added largely to the garden, and took in two acres more of land, and planted a row of Elms and Beech trees. She kept the garden as bright and gay as the samplers she worked herself. She had a mania for set beds, and her Tulips were the talk of the county. A long bed of them ran from the house along one bank of the bowling-green to the orchard, and it was arranged in pattern of colours, lines, squares, interlaced geometrical designs of flaming red and scarlet, pink and yellow and white and dull purple. She it was who caused the sundial to be placed in the garden and who found the motto for it, and designed the four triangular beds to go round it, and placed a hedge of Lavender and Rosemary all about it in a square.

The tap of her stick on the paths is one of the ghostly sounds that haunt the place, and sometimes it is difficult to know whether it is a woodpecker, or a thrush breaking open a snail, or her stick that makes such a sharp crisp sound on the Summer air.

There is another sound, too, that the Acacia tree knows well. It is the click of glasses under its boughs. On a table placed under the tree is an array of beautiful cut-glass decanters and a number of glasses which reflect in the polished mahogany surface. Round the table four gentlemen sit with white wigs and elegant lace falls at their throats, and ruffles at their wrists. It is a hot Summer afternoon, and so still that not a Rose leaf of those spread on the lawn stirs. A large white sheet lies on the lawn covered with thousands of rose petals left to dry in the sun, and when they are dry, and have undergone a careful mixture with spices, and have herbs added to them by the mistress of the house, they will be placed in china bowls in all the rooms, and will give out a subtle delicious odour.

The man who is dreaming in his garden can see the four gentlemen as plain as life raising their glasses and touch them before drinking the silent toast. And it is difficult to tell whether it is the gardener striking on his frames by accident, or the chink of glasses that sounds so clearly under the Acacia tree.

Now, in another picture the garden holds, things are somewhat altered. Instead of the big Tulip bed on the lawn there are a number of small cut beds with long beds behind them on either side of a new gravel walk. Instead of the older fashioned borders there are startling colour schemes of carpet-bedding in which the flowers are made to look more like coloured earths than anything. In the long beds, instead of the profusion of Hollyhocks, Sunflowers and bushes of Roses, a primness reigns. A row of blue Lobelia backed by a row of white Lobelia, then scarlet Geraniums, then Calceolarias, then crimson Beet plants, every ten yards a Marguerite Daisy sticks up out of the middle of the bed. Only one rambling border remains, and that is hidden from the view of the house windows, but can just be seen from the seat under the Acacia tree. In it Phlox and Red-hot Pokers, Asters, Anemonies, Moss Rose, and French

172

Marigolds grow profusely, and some merciful sentiment has allowed an old twisted Apple tree to remain there.

The old bowling-green is still beautifully kept, the grass is smooth and fair, not a Daisy or Plantain is there to mar the splendour of the turf. The Acacia tree, now grown old and venerable, spreads out fine branches, and gives delightful shade. Here and there new arches of rustic woodwork, in horrible designs, stretch over the paths, their ugliness partly hidden by climbing Roses of the Seven Sisters kind, or Clematis, or Honeysuckle, or Jasmine. Many trees in the garden are old enough to exchange memories of a hundred years ago ; the orchard alone boasts a venerable congregation of old trees, some grey with lichen, some bowed down with the result of full crops.

New ghosts walk the garden paths in crinolines and Leghorn hats, and side curls, talking to gentlemen with glossy side whiskers, peg-top trousers, and tartan waist-coats.

On the bowling-green the new game is laid out, and ladies and gentlemen talk learnedly of bisques, and the correct weight of croquet mallets. There is a fresh sound for the garden, the smack of croquet balls.

And now nearly all the ghosts vanish, and the old man who is sitting under the Acacia tree looks around and sees his garden as it is to-day, fuller of flowers than ever it was, with the hideous set borders done away with, with the little rustic arches pulled down and a pergola, properly built, in their place, and all of the horrors of Early Victorian gardening gone for good, the plaster nymphs and cupids, the tree called a " Monkey Puzzler," the terrible rockery of clinkers and bad bricks. Here, as in the house, taste has triumphed over fashion. Inside the oak panels that had been covered over with hideous wallpapers are brought to light. The wool mats have vanished, the glass domes over clocks, the worsted bell-pulls, the druggets and the rep curtains all gone for good.

Outside, wonders have been worked in the garden. New beds filled with the choicest Roses and Carnations. Water is now properly conveyed by a sprinkler. The old water-butt, slimy and falling to pieces, gone to give place to a well filled concrete tank of water, kept clean and sweet.

One more ghostly sound left, a sound the lonely man unconsciously listens for as he sits under the tree. On one bough, low growing and strong, shows the marks deep cut where once depended the ropes of a swing. In his ears he can sometimes hear the shouts of children and the creak of the swing ropes, sounds he used to hear in his childhood. And mingled with the children's laughter he can hear, very faintly, a boy's voice, his own.

Such is the story of an hundred English Gardens, where trees will tell secrets, and the lawn holds memories, and the paths echo with footsteps out of the past.

*   *   *   *   *

The influence literature has on the mind is nowhere more traceable than in a garden. A dozen thoughts spring to the mind gathered out of the store cupboards of remembered reading at the sight of flowers, trees, sunlit walks, dark alleys. Trees call up romantic meetings, hollow trunks where lovers have posted their letters, dark shades where vows have been made, smooth trunks on which are carven twin hearts pierced by a single arrow and crowned with initials cut into the bark. Gloomy recesses under spreading boughs remind one of the hiding places of conspirators, of fugitives.

Sometimes, on a winter's night, to look into the garden and see the trees toss and shake with an angry wind, or stand bare, bleak, and black against the sparkle of a

174

frosty sky, some written thing comes quickly into the brain almost as if the printed letters stood out clear. There is one scene of winter and trees comes often to me very full and clear. It is from the beginning of " Martin Chuzzlewit," and heralds the entrance in the story of the immortal Mr. Pecksniff.

" The fallen leaves, with which the ground was strewn, gave forth a pleasant fragrance, and, subduing all harsh sounds of distant feet and wheels, created a repose in gentle unison with the light scattering of seed hither and thither by the distant husbandman, and with the noiseless passage of the plough as it turned up the rich brown earth and wrought a graceful pattern in the stubbled fields. On the motionless branches of some trees autumn berries hung like clusters of coral beads, as in those fabled orchards where the fruits were jewels ; others, stripped of all their garniture, stood, each the centre of its little heap of bright red leaves, watching their slow decay ; others again still wearing theirs, had them all crunched and crackled up, as though they had been burnt. About the stems of some were piled, in ruddy mounds, the apples they had borne that year ; while others (hardy evergreens this class) showed somewhat stern and gloomy in their vigour, as charged by nature with the admonition that it is not to her more sensitive and joyous favourites she grants the longest term of life. Still athwart their darker boughs the sunbeams struck out paths of deeper gold ; and the red light, mantling in among their swarthy branches, used them as foils to set its brightness off, and aid the lustre of the dying day.

" A moment, and its glory was no more. The sun went down beneath the long dark lines of hill and cloud which piled up in the west an airy city, wall heaped on wall, and battlement on battlement ; the light was

175

all withdrawn; the shining church turned cold and dark; the stream forgot to smile; the birds were silent; and the gloom of winter dwelt in everything.

"An evening wind uprose too, and the slighter branches cracked and rattled as they moved, in skeleton dances, to its moaning music. The withering leaves, no longer quiet, hurried to and fro in search of shelter from its chill pursuit; the labourer unyoked the horses, and, with head bent down, trudged briskly home beside them; and from the cottage windows lights began to glance and wink upon the darkening fields.

* * * * *

"It was small tyranny for a respectable wind to go wreaking its vengeance on such poor creatures as the fallen leaves; but this wind, happening to come up with a great heap of them just after venting its humour on the insulted Dragon, did so disperse and scatter them that they fled away, pell-mell, some here, some there, rolling over each other, whirling round and round upon their thin edges, taking frantic flights into the air, and playing all manner of extraordinary gambols in the extremity of their distress. Nor was this good enough for its malicious fury; for not content with driving them abroad, it charged small parties of them, and hunted them into the wheelrights saw-pit, and below the planks and timbers in the yard, and, scattering the sawdust in the air it looked for them underneath, and when it did meet with any, whew! how it drove them on and followed on their heels!

"The scared leaves only flew the faster for all this, and a giddy chase it was; for they got into unfrequented places, where there was no outlet, and where their pursuer kept them eddying round and round at his pleasure; and they crept under the eaves of houses, and clung tightly to the sides of hayricks like bats;

176

and tore in at open chamber windows, and cowered close to hedges; and, in short, went anywhere for safety. But the oddest feat they achieved was, to take advantage of the sudden opening of Mr. Pecksniff's front door, to dash wildly down his passage, with the wind following close upon them, and finding the back door open, incontinently blew out the lighted candle held by Miss Pecksniff, and slammed the front door against Mr. Pecksniff, who was at that moment entering, with such violence, that in the twinkling of an eye, he lay on his back at the bottom of the steps. Being by this time weary of such trifling performances, the boisterous rover hurried away rejoicing, roaring over moor and meadow, hill and flat, until it got out to sea, where it met with other winds similarly disposed, and made a night of it."

*   *   *   *   *

Is not this wonderful and immortal passage as much a part of the Charm of Gardens as the most delectable poetry on the perfumed air of a summer night?

Often, when the logs are crackling on the hearth, one hears those hunted leaves come banging on the window panes, those gaunt trees tossing in the wind. When all the garden lies cold and bare and stripped of green, the trees roar out an answer to the wind, an hundred garden voices swell the storm, and you sit happy by your fireside and dream new colours for the garden beds; and where a white frost sparkles on the earth, and trees lift up bare fingers to the sky, you see deep wealth of green, and jewelled borders brim full of spring flowers, and there a set of bulbs you have nursed, come out sweet in green sheathes, and here a tree, now naked, clothed in young green.

That for the night. For the morning, trailing clouds of mist over the trees like fairy shawls alive with dew-

177

diamonds, each dew-drop reflecting its tiny world. The trees, the world, the garden still asleep, or half asleep, until the sun throws off the counterpane of clouds and springs into the skies.

It is at that time, before the sun is awake, the trees look strange as sleeping things look strange, with a counterfeit of death, so still are they. And in the Spring when the orchard is a pale ghost before the sun is up, a man would swear it had been covered up at night in silver smoke, or gossamer, or fairy silk that the sun tears into weeping shreds that drip and drip and give the grass a bath.

But of the effect of trees as a spiritual support no man is at variance with another. That they give courage, and help and hope, that the green sight of them is good as being reminder that Heaven is kind, and that the Winter is not always, no man doubts but, perhaps, fears to voice, feeling his neighbour will call out at him for a worshipper of Pan and of strange gods. But to the garden dweller, or to him who must perforce make his garden of one tree in a dusty court, and of one glass of flowers on his desk, these things have voices, and they are kindly voices, saying, " Despair not," and " Regard me how I grow upright through the seasons," and also " Give shade and shelter to all things and men equally as I do, without distinction or difference, and if the grass gives a couch, fair and embroidered with flowers, so do I give a roof of infinite variety, and a shade from the sun, and a shelter from the wind." And again, " If a man know a tree to love it he will understand much of men, and of birds, and beasts and of all living things. And of greater things too, for in the branches is other fruit than the fruit of the tree. Just as the rainbow is set in the sky for a promise, so is fruit in a tree set there ; and the leaves show how orderly is the Great Plan ; and the

178

branches show the strength of slender things, and of little things, so that a man may know how Heaven has its roots in earth, and its crest in the clouds.   And a man who holds to earth with one hand, and reaches at the stars with the other, in that span he encompasses all that may be known if he but see it.   But men are blind, and do not see the sky but as sky, and do not see the stars but as balls of fire, or the green grass but as a carpet, or the flowers but as a combination of chemical accidents.   But over all, and through all, and in all is God, Who still speaks with Adam in the Garden."

These things are to be learnt of trees both great and small, withered and young, sapling and Oak of centuries. And they are to be learnt also in the dust on a butterfly's wing ; or of a blade of grass ; or of a hemp seed.   But men are deaf, and hear no voice but the voice of water in a rushing stream ; and no sound but the sound of leaves stirring when the wind rests in a tree ; and no voice speaking in a blaze of flowers who sing praises night and day in scented voices.

A tree is not dumb, and the Creeping Briar is not dumb, and the Rose has a voice like the voice of a woman rejoicing that she is fair.   But men are dumb, for though their hearts speak, all tongues are not touched with fire.

So may trees be a solace in trouble, and secrets may be whispered to bushes of Rosemary and Lavender, who will yield their secret solace of peace, as the tree yields strength.   All these things are written in a garden in coloured letters of gold, and green, and crimson, in blue and purple, orange and grey, and they are written for a purpose.   And a man may seek diligently for the secret of this great book and find nothing if he seek with his head alone.   He will tell of the growth of trees, their years, their nature, their sickness.   He will learn of the power of the sap which flows down from the tips of leaves to the great tree roots all snug in the soil ; and he will learn of the veins in the leaves, and the properties of the gum of the bark, yet will he never learn that of which the tree speaks always, night and day—praising.

Of what is the colour of green that the earth's best page is made of it ? Of what is the colour of young green that it brings, unbidden, tender thoughts ? It is more than the gold of Corn, and the brown of ploughed earth, and the glory of flowers. By it comes peace to the eyes, and through the eyes to the heart of man, so that men say of youth and the times of youth that they are salad days ; and of old age, if so be it is a fine old age, that it is green. It is the colour of the body as blue is the colour of the soul. The sky and the sea are blue, and they are things of mystery, deep and profound, and because of their great depth and profundity they are blue. The grass and the trees, and the leaves of flowers, and blades of young Corn are green. They are mysterious things but they are nearer to man, and he has them to his hand to be near them, and get quick comfort of them.

And Daisies are the stars of the grass, as stars are the Daisies of Heaven ; and if a man look long at the stars set out orderly in the sky he may become fearful, for God may seem far off and difficult ; yet if he be near he may pick a Daisy and take his fill of comfortable things, for God will seem near and His voice in the Daisy.

Yet many a man will walk over a field of grass pressing the Daisies with his feet, and take no heed of them, or of the stars over above his head ; and the night and the day will be to him but light and darkness, and the stars but lanterns to show him home, and the Daisies but flowers of the field. But if he be a man who sees all, and in everything can feel the finger and pulse of God, his staff will blossom in his hand, and he will go on his way rejoicing.

180

THE EFFECT OF TREES

In this way can man regard the trees in his garden, and speak with them, loving them, and learning of them, for learning is all of love.　And he may yet be an ordinary man, not poet, or artist, but he must be mystic because he has the true sight.　Many a man, stockbroker, clerk, painter, labourer, soldier, or whatever he seems to be, has his real being in these moments, and they are revealed through love or sorrow, but not by hard learning or text-books.

III

A LOVER OF GARDENS

THERE are many who say this and that of Sir John Mandeville, his Travels ; that he was not ; that he was a Frenchman ; that no one knows who he was. For years he was to me an English Knight who lived at St. Albans, and from there set out to travel over all the world seeking adventure, and relating the peculiarities of his journey in fascinating, if slightly imaginative, language. I rejoiced when he saw a board from the Noah's Ark, when he talked with the Cham of Tartary ; and told of the wonders of Ind. But comes along this and that expert who upset the figure of the gallant Knight, and heave him from horse to ground as a dummy figure, and burn him for firewood as a fallen idol. And why ? It appears that Sir John is no more a real being than Homer, or Æsop, or any other of those personal names for great bundles of collected literature ; and is a literature all by himself, and a series of impudent thieves who stole travellers' tales and jotted them together in a personal narrative. For all that I believe in a figure of the blind Homer, and the impudent slave Æsop who played tricks on his master, and I firmly believe in a stalwart figure of Sir John Mandeville, Knight, " albeit," he says, " I be not worthy, that was born in England, in the town of St. Albans, and passed the sea in the year of our Lord Jesu Christ, 1322, in the day of St. Michael."

There is one thing, a touch of character, put in, maybe, by the skilful editor of these travels, that makes us lean to the man as being a real person. It is his love of Gardens, and his pains to tell of them, and the stories of trees, and legends. And whether one who confessed to the fraud of putting these travels together—Jean de Bourgogne, by name—was a keen gardener or herbalist, or whether it was a literary habit of the fourteenth century (which, when I come to think of it, is so), somehow I feel that there is a garden-loving spirit in forming the book, and for that I love the man.

In his wanderings Sir John meets many things, and of these I beg leave to choose here and there one or two of his anecdotes when they touch an idea such as gardeners love. The first is of the True Cross, and the story of its origin. All of Sir John I have read in Mr. Pollard's edition, than which nothing could be more satisfactory and clear expressed.

Of the Cross

" And the Christian men, that dwell beyond the sea, in Greece, say that the Tree of the Cross, that we call Cypress, was one of that tree that Adam ate the apple off ; and that find they written. And they say also, that their Scripture saith, that Adam was sick, and said to his son Seth, that he should go to the angel that kept Paradise, that he would send him the oil of mercy, for to anoint with his members, that he might have health. And Seth went. But the angel would not let him come in ; but said to him, that he might not have of the oil of mercy. But he took him three grains of the same tree, that his father ate the apple off ; and bade him, a soon as his father was dead, that he should put these three grains under his tongue, and grave him so ; and so he did. And of these three grains sprang a tree, as the angel said it should, and bare a fruit, through the which fruit Adam should be saved.

" And when Seth came again, he found his father near dead. And when he was dead, he did with the grains as the angel bade him ; of the which sprung three trees, of the which the Cross was made, that bare good fruit and blessed, our Lord Jesu Christ."

OF THE CROWN OF THORNS

" AND if all it be so, that men say, that this crown is of thorns, ye shall understand that, it was of jonkes of the sea, that is to say, rushes of the sea, that prick as sharply as thorns.   For I have seen and beholden many times that of Paris and that of Constantinople ; for they were both one, made of rushes of the sea.   But man have departed them in two parts : of the which one part is at Paris, and the other part is at Constantinople.   And I have one of those precious thorns that seemeth like a White Thorn ; and that was given to me for great speciality.   For there are many of them broken and fallen into the vessel that the crown lieth in ; for they break for dryness when the men move them to show to great lords that come hither.

" And ye shall understand, that our Lord Jesu, in that night that he was taken, he was led into a garden ; and there he was first examined right sharply ; and there the Jews scorned him, and made him a crown of the branches of the Albespine, that is White Thorn, that grew in that same garden, and set it on his head, so fast and so sore, that the blood ran down by many places of his visage, and of his neck, and of his shoulders.   And therefore hath the White Thorn many virtues, for he that beareth a branch on him thereof, no thunder or no manner of tempest may dere him ; nor in the house that it is in may no evil ghost enter nor come into the place

185

that it is in. And in that same garden, Saint Peter denied our Lord thrice.

" Afterward was our Lord led forth before the bishops and the masters of the law, into another garden of Annas ; and there also he was examined, reproved, and scorned, and crowned eft with a Sweet Thorn, that men clepeth Barbarines, that grew in that garden, and that hath also many virtues.

" And after he was led into a garden of Caiphas, and then he was crowned with Aglantine.

" And after he was led into the chamber of Pilate, and there he was examined and crowned. And the Jews set him in a chair, and clad him in a mantle ; and there made they the crown of jonkes of the sea ; and there they kneeled to him, and scorned him, saying, ' Ave, Rex Judeoram ! ' That is to say, ' Hail, King of Jews ! ' And of this crown, half is at Paris, and the other half at Constantinople."

*   *   *   •   *

From these fanciful byways Sir John goes on his way looking, as before, for curious things, and for marvels of trees and fruits. He tells of the fine plate of gold writ by Hermogenes, the wise man who foretold the birth of Christ. He passes the Isles of Colcos and of Lango where the daughter of Ypocras is yet in the form of a dragon. And he goes by the town of Jaffa—" for one of the sons of Noah, that bright Japhet, founded it, and now it is called Joppa. And ye shall understand, that it is one of the oldest towns of the world, for it was founded before Noah's flood. And yet there sheweth in the rock, there as the iron chains were fastened, that Andromeda, a great giant was bounden with, and put in prison before Noah's flood, of the which giant, is a rib of his side that is forty foot long."

Then he finds in Egypt some curious Apples.

V

OF APPLES

"ALSO in that country and in others also, men find long Apples to sell, in their season, and men clepe them Apples of Paradise; and they be right sweet and of good savour. And though ye cut them in never so many gobbets or parts, over-thwart or endlong, ever-more ye shall find in the midst the figure of the Holy Cross of our Lord Jesu.

*   *   *   *   *

"And men find there also the Apple of the tree of Adam, that have a bite at one of the sides; and there be also small Fig trees that bear no leaves, but Figs upon the small branches; and men clepe them Figs of Pharoah."

Sir John, on his constant look out lets no oddment pass him by, and the more peculiar the better. It appears he would rather see a well in a field—"that our Lord Jesu Christ made with one of his feet, when he went to play with other children "—than many things political or notable to the country. And he will never come to a country but he will mention the state of its trees and fruits, these, naturally, being important items to the traveller of his day who might at any moment have to fall back on the natural fruits of the field for his food. So, when he goes by the desert to the valley of Elim, he notes the seventy-two

187

Palm trees there growing—" the which Moses found with the children of Israel."

Then he comes by Mount Sinai, and there he finds the convent by the spot where was the burning bush ; and the Church of Saint Catherine is there—" in the which be many lamps burning; for they have of oil of Olives enough, both to burn in their lamps and to eat also. And that plenty they have by the miracle of God ; for the raven and the crows and the choughs and other fowls of the country assemble them there every year once, and fly thither as in pilgrimage ; and everych of them bringeth a branch of the Bays or of the Olive in their beaks instead of offering, and leave them there ; of which the monks make great plenty of oil. And this is a great marvel."

VI

OF THE FIRST GARDENER

Now Sir John, who had a great feeling for our first
father Adam, came frequently on stories of him and of
places where he lived. And he went from Bathsheba,
the town founded, as he says—" by Bersabe, the wife of
Sir Uriah the Knight,"—and journeyed to the city of
Hebron. " And it was clept sometime the Vale of
Mamre, and sometimes it was clept the Vale of Tears,
because that Adam wept there an hundred year for the
death of Abel his son, that Cain slew."

There, in this Vale of Hebron, where Sir John says
Abraham had his house, and is buried, as are Adam and
Eve, Isaac, Jacob, Sarah, Leah, and Rebecca, is also the
first dwelling-place of Adam after the Fall.

" And right fast by that place is a cave in the rock,
where Adam and Eve dwelled when they were put out of
Paradise ; and there got they their children. And in the
same place was Adam formed and made, after that some
men say (for men were wont for to clept that place the
field of Damascus, because that it was in the lordship of
Damascus), and from thence he was translated into
Paradise of delights, as they say ; and after that he was
driven out of Paradise he was there left. And the same
day that he was put in Paradise, the same day he was
put out, for anon he sinned. There beginneth the Vale
of Hebron, that dureth nigh to Jerusalem. There the
Angel commanded Adam that he should dwell with his

189

wife Eve, of the which he gat Seth ; of which tribe, that is to say kindred, Jesu Christ was born."

*   *   *   *   *

Here then is the legend of the first Garden in which Adam delved, and lived by the sweat of his brow. Again Sir John tells us of a place where he noticed the trees, especially the Dry tree, and it can be seen how much a lover of Gardens and of growing things he was, and how he looked for and noticed these things and set them down.

This Dry Tree was an Oak of Abraham's time.

OR THE DRY TREE

" And there is a tree of Oak, that the Saracens clepe Dirpe, that is of Abraham's time ; the which men clepe the Dry tree.   And they say that it hath been there since the beginning of the world, and was some-time green and bare leaves, until the time that our Lord died on the Cross, and then it dried ; and so did all the trees that were then in the world.   And some say, by their prophecies, that a lord, a prince of the west side of the world, shall win the Land of Promission, that is the Holy Land, with the help of Christian men, and he shall do sing a mass under that Dry tree ; and then the tree shall wax green, and bear both fruit and leaves, and through that miracle many Saracens and Jews shall be turned to Christian faith ; and, therefore, they do great worship thereto, and keep it full busily.   And, albeit so, that it dry, natheles yet he beareth great virtue, for certainly he hath a little thereof upon him, it healeth him of the falling evil, and his horse shall not be afoundered : and many other virtues it hath ; wherefore men hold it full precious."

190

VII

OF THE FIRST ROSES

THEN Sir John tells of a field nigh to Bethlehem, called Floridus, and here was a maiden wrongfully blamed, and condemned to death, and to be burnt.

"And as the fire began to burn about her, she made her prayers to our Lord, that as wisely as she was not guilty of that sin, that he would keep her and make it to be known to all men, of His merciful grace. And when she had thus said, she entered into the fire, and anon was the fire quenched and out ; and the brands that were burning became red Rose trees, and the brands that were not kindled became white Rose trees, full of Roses. And these were the first Rose trees and Roses, both white and red, that every any man said ; and thus was this maiden saved by the grace of God. And therefore is that field clept the Field of God Flourished, for it was full of Roses."

*　　*　　*　　*　　*

And later Sir John tells how he saw the Elder tree on the which Judas hanged himself. And he tells of the Sycamore tree that Zaccheus the dwarf climbed into. And of a plank of Noah's ship that a monk, by the Grace of God, brought down from Ararat.

Then Sir John comes to Java on his wanderings, and by that isle is another called Pathen, and here he saw wonderful trees, bearing bread, and honey, and wine, and poison. Of the tree that bears the venom he says :

"And other trees that bear venom, against which

191

there is no medicine, but one ; and that is to take their proper leaves and stamp them and temper them with water, and then drink it, and else he shall die ; for triacle will not avail, ne none other medicine. Of this venom the Jews had let seek of one of their friends for to empoison all Christianity, as I have heard them say in their confession before their dying ; but thank be to Almighty God ! they failed of their purpose ; but always they make great mortality of people."

Yet again Sir John has marvels of other countries, where are men who—" when their friends be sick they hang them upon trees, and say that it is better that birds that be angels of God eat them, than the foul worms of the earth."

And near by is the isle of Calonak, where gardeners would indeed be evily distressed by reason of the snail—" that be so great, that many persons may lodge them in their shells, as men would do in a little house."

By taking ship Sir John goes from isle to isle discussing the sights, and arrives at length at an isle where—" be white hens without feathers, but they bear white wool as sheep do here " ; and he passes by Cassay, of the greatest cities of the world, and goes from that city by water to an abbey of monks.

VIII

OF THE ABBEY GARDEN

" From that city men go by water, solacing and disporting them, till they come to an abbey of monks that is fast by, that be good religious men after their faith and law.

" In that abbey is a great garden and fair, where be many trees of diverse manner of fruits. And in this garden is a little hill full of delectable trees. In that hill and in that garden be many diverse beasts, as of apes, marmosets, baboons, and many other diverse beasts. And every day, when the convent of this abbey hath eaten, the almoner let bear the relief to the garden, and he smiteth on the garden gate with a clicket of silver that he holdeth in his hand ; and anon all the beasts of the hill and of the diverse places of the garden come out a 3,000 or a 4,000 ; and they come in guise of poor men, and men give them the relief in fair vessels of silver, clean over-gilt. And when they have eaten, the monk smiteth efftsoons on the garden gate with the clicket, and then anon all the beasts return again to their places that they come from.

" And they say that these beasts be souls of worthy men that resemble in likeness of those beasts that be fair, and therefore they give them meat for the love of God ; and the other beasts that be foul, they say be souls of poor men and of rude commons."

*   *   *   *   *

Many other marvels did Sir John see, of which I shall not tell ; but he writes always with his eye open and easy for miracles,and talks as a gardener talks of strange flowers and fruit, as of gourds that when they be ripe— " men cut them a-two, and men find within a little beast, in flesh, and bone and blood, as though it were a little lamb without wool. And men eat both the fruit and the beast. And that is a great marvel." Then he writes of the wonders of the country of Prester John, and of trees there that men dare not eat of the fruit—" for it is a thing of faerie."

Of Gatholonabes, he writes, and of the sham Garden of Eden he made, and of the birds that—" sing full delectably and moved by craft." The fairest garden any man might behold it was. And of the men and girls clothed in cloths of gold full richly, that he said were angels.

And of Paradise he cannot speak, making towards the end of the book confession.

" Of Paradise ne can I not speak properly. For I was not there. It is far beyond. And that forthinketh me. And also I was not worthy."

And so, after a little more, ends Sir John, and so I end, though I love him. Yet I doubt some of his stories.

IX

THE OLYMPIAN ASPECT

THERE are many ways of regarding a garden of flowers ; from the utilitarian view it is a reasonable method of utilising a space of ground for horticultural purposes, but I prefer to take the Olympian view and quote from " The Poet's Geography," to the effect that a garden of flowers is—" A collection of dreams surrounded by clouds."

At first sight the somewhat expansive imagery of this definition might appear over-vague and unsatisfactory where a very definite question, like a garden of flowers, is concerned. But, come to see it in a lofty light, and at once its truth stands clear. A garden is the proper adjunct of a house, and a house, fully said, is a dream come true, yet still surrounded by the clouds of infinite possibilities. It is always growing, is a true home. Like a flower it expands to every sweet whisper of the wind. Like a flower it shuts at night, or opens to accept the dew. It is something so elusive that only the garlands of love hold it together.

The garden, to the real house, is, like the dwelling, a place of the most subtle fancies. Every flower there, every tree and each blade of grass holds mystery and imagination. The Gods walk there.

The flower beds (accepting the Olympian idea) are not mere collections of flowering herbage, but are volumes of poetry growing in the sun. Take your hedge of Sweet Peas, for example, and tell me what they are—no—tell

195

me who they are. There is a dream there if you like ;
and while you look at them, and sniff them delicately, is
not the fussy world shut off from you by clouds. Sweet
Peas are like a bevy of winsome girls all in their everyday
frocks, scented by an odour of virginity, something in-
describably refined after the manner of the flesh, and
something lofty in their removal from the earth after the
way of the spirit. I wonder how many people feel this.

Take it more broadly in the true Olympian spirit.
Take it that a house and garden is an Olympus to each
man and woman who is happy, and you will see that your
heaven for all its head in the clouds has its feet upon the
earth. Then what do the flowers mean ? Lilies with
pale faces like a procession of nuns. Roses all queens of
regal beauty. Violets to whom the thrushes sing, deny
it if you dare. Majestic Peonies. The plants of soft
and courtly wisdom, Thyme, Rosemary, Myrtle. Lavender, the House-dame, prim, neat, beloved of bees and
butterflies, Quakerishly dressed in grey with a touch of
unsectarian colour, yet vaguely an ecclesiastical purple ;
rather slim, with full skirts, with the suggestion that
Cowslips are her bunches of keys, and the Dandelion her
clock.

One could go on for ever.

And then the gardener, like those half-immortals who
worked for the gods, or some like a god of old, even, with
god-like grumbles, and god-like simplicity.

They are a strange race, these gardeners, given to
unexpected meals, and sudden appearances.

" Walter ! "

And after that, from some fragrant bush, or waving
forest of Asparagus, a bronzed man stands erect, as if he
had sprung from the bowels of the earth, where he had
been contemplating the mysteries of human weakness.

And how amazed they are with us and our foibles and

196

follies. We remonstrate—a question of weeds, perhaps,
—and are listened to with incredulous wonder.

" Weeds ! " says the being, " weeds ! "

He emerges more completely from the bush, showing a
hand occupied with a lot of little twigs, and a knife rather
like himself to look at—not too sharp.

As if a voice from the unknown had wafted over the
desert, he stands in wonder, looking reproachfully at
those who have interrupted his toil.

" The weather makes them grow." Of course it does.
We knew that. We did not come here to call Walter
to ask him what made weeds grow, but to know why he
had not weeded, at our special request, the Carnation
border.

From a cavernous pocket in a much-mended pair of
trousers of a shape never designed by mortal hands, he
produces a quantity of felt strips, and some wall nails.

We repeat our original suggestion, that the Carnation
border is choked with weeds.

" So it be ! "

Then, after the great being has taken observations of
the sky, causing him to screw up one eye and wag his
head sagely as if he had communication with the unseen
powers, he admits that he has been watering the green-
house.

" The Vines take a deal o' time about now."

It would be useless to remark to this calm person that
we found, only yesterday, a dozen plants dying in the
greenhouse, and all for want of water. But, from a sort
of foolhardy courage, we do say as much.

" Yes," says the immortal, " they need a power of
water. A good drop is no good."

We venture to remonstrate with him, saying, in a few
well chosen words, that it would be useful of him, then,
to give them " a good watering while he was about it."

He agrees at once. " It would do them a power of good."

Realising that we are drifting from the main grievance, we return hot to the bed of Carnations. We admit to having but just this moment come from weeding them ourselves, and in so saying we hope to make appeal to his better nature. Nothing of the kind.

" I noticed," he says, " you sp'iled some of the layers where you'd a-been treading."

When we have turned away defeated, he sinks again to his mysterious task, and it seems that the ground swallows him.

Then again, in the early morning, he seems to have had overnight talks with Mercury, or Apollo, or whoever it is who arranges the weather, as he invariably greets us with some curt sentence.

" Rain afore noon," or " Wind'll be in the nor'west afore night." Thereby giving us to understand that he has been given a glass of nectar in some lower servants' hall in Olympus, and has picked up the gossip of what Jupiter has decreed for the day. We feel, as he intends us to feel, vastly inferior. In fact we have given way to a habit of asking his advice on certain points, which has proved fatal.

He doles out our fruit to us just as he likes, and we feel quite guilty when we pick one of our own peaches from our own walls.

" I see you pick a peach last night," he says. " 'Tisn't for me to say anything, but I was countin' on giving you a nice dish NEXT week."

What is there to do but hang one's head, and plead guilty ?

Boys are his pet aversion. Whether boys have in some way a fellowship with the gods (which I suspect), or whether they are victoriously antagonistic, it matters

198

not. They are to the gardener so many creatures whom he classes along with snails, bullfinches, rabbits and wasps as " varmints."

One can hear him sometimes invoking a god of the name of Gum. " By Gum ! them young varmints a-been 'ere again. By Gum ! "

He then makes an offering to this god in the shape of a bonfire, the smell of which is more than most scents for wonder.

It is when Walter makes a bonfire that he is more god-like than ever. He stands, a thick figure, deep in the chest, broad in the shoulder, by the pile of dead leaves, twigs, and garden rubbish, the smoke enveloping him in misty wreaths, and the sun flashing on his fork as he pitches fresh fuel on the smouldering fire. A tongue of flame, greedily licking up leaves and dry sticks, lights on his impassive face, and a quivering orange streak along the muscles of his arms. We are fascinated by his arms. They contain, I believe, the history of his mortal life and ambitions, and are a key to his hidden emotions.

On one arm is a ship under full sail, done in blue and red tattoo. Below the ship is the word " Jane " ; below that is a twist of rope. On the other arm is a heart, the initials S.M., and an anchor.

When we were young these two arms of Walter's were an entire literature to us. We read him first, I think, a pirate, very grim and horrible, and we translated " S.M." as Spanish Main. A little later we dropped the idea of the pirate, and took to the notion that Walter had been (if he was not still) a smuggler who landed cargoes of rum from the good ship " Jane," and deposited them with the landlord of the " Saucy Mariner." It is noticeable that we left out the heart in all these romances. Then, at some impressionable moment, Walter became a seaman who had given his heart to Sarah Mainwaring, which name we got from a man who had given us a dog, and in spite of that we accepted it as fact. I think we once descended so low as to think that the whole thing had no nautical significance, and was a secret sign of some terrible society who met for purposes of revenge. This, of course, was the result of contemporary reading.

Then came the great day upon which Walter was definitely asked what the signs and pictures on his arms did mean.

" Mind out," was all the answer we got, and Walter retired with the wheelbarrow to his citadel—the potting shed.

It was tried again a little later, and this time met with a little better response, because, I suppose, we had done more than half his day's work for him.

" I had them done at a fair."

" And," we asked breathlessly, " what was the ship ? "

" Two shillin's," he replied, " and I never regretted it. Money well spent."

" Was she your ship ? "

" Mine ? " said the god.

" Was she the ship you were in when you were a sailor ? "

" Me ? " said Walter. " I aint never been a sailor."

The blow was crushing. We retired hurt, amazed, incredulous.

One day we tried the remaining arm, the one with S.M., the heart, and the anchor emblazoned on it.

" What does S.M. mean ? "

It was a moment of terrific suspense. We had drawn a mental picture of some wonderful creature, half Princess, half like a schoolgirl, we sighed after. The god was tying Carnations to wire spirals, and his expression was limited, since he had a knife in his mouth.

" S.M. on me arm," he said, removing the knife.

200

THE OLYMPIAN ASPECT

We nodded mysteriously, full of breathless expectation.

Walter began to smile. He stood up and surveyed us with his face alight with the memory of some great day. To us he looked an heroic figure, even despite the pieces of old drawing-room carpet tied to his knees with string, and his very unkempt beard.

" You won't exactly understand," he said, mopping his forehead. " But I tell 'ee if you've got to mind some-at after a day at a fair, you'd be fair mazed. I give my word to my mother as I'd a-put sixpence in a raffle for to try to win her a sewing machine, and so when the fellow was making they images on my arm, I sed to un, I sed, put me S.M., I sed, so's I'll mind to put in the sewing machine raffle, I sed, or else if so be as I don't I shall get a slice of tongue pie when I do get home along."

Our faces fell. Our hearts, full of romance, now became like lead. In despair we put the last question, a forlorn hope in the storming of his heart's citadel.

" And the other thing on your arms, Walter ? The heart."

" Cooriosity killed a monkey," said he. " Mind out, I'm going round the corners."

So was our romance killed. " Going round the corners," was Walter's sign that all conversation was closed.

If one followed him " round the corners," talk as one might, Walter directed all his conversation to the flowers. To hear him address the plants in the greenhouse was to think him indeed a god, who by some magic spell turned the water in the can into a life-saving potion. To-day we think that much of the soliloquy was done for our especial benefit.

" Just a wee drop, my pretty," he would say to some

201

flower. " Just a drink with lunch. That's right. Perk up now. By Gum, you do want your drop regular, you 'ardened teetotaler. Hello, hello, what's up with you ? Looks to me as if a snail had bided along o' you too frequent."

His great hand, covered with ancient scars, would lift the leaves tenderly, and search beneath for the offending snail which, when found, would be held up to view.

" Five-and-twenty tailors ! " he would exclaim.

He would be instantly corrected. " Four-and-twenty."

" You got your history wrong," he used to say.

We repeated

Four-and-twenty tailors went to catch a snail,
And the best man among them dare not touch his tail.

" Come the twenty-fifth," Walter added. " That be I. So here goes, Master Snail."

With that the snail was sharply crushed underfoot, and the soliloquy continued. He is with us still, older in years, younger than ever in heart, with the same immortal personality, the same atmosphere of friendship with the gods about him. He listens to orders with a smile of amusement, just as if he had been laughing about our ways only an hour before with some inhabitant of an unseen world. He carried his own peculiar atmosphere with him of indulgent superiority and warm-heartedness combined, just as the tortoise carries his house on his back. If that story is unknown by any chance, here it is.

JUPITER'S WEDDING

When the toy had once taken Jupiter in the head to enter into a state of matrimony, he resolved for the honour of his Celestial Lady, that the whole world should keep a Festival upon the day of his marriage, and so invited all living creatures, Tag-Rag and Bob-Tail, to the solemnity of his wedding. They all came in very good time, saving only the Tortoise. Jupiter told him 'twas ill done to make the Company stay, and asked him, " Why so late ? " " Why truly," says the Tortoise, " I was at home, at my own House, my dearly beloved House," and House is Home, let it be never so Homely. Jupiter took it very ill at his hands, that he should think himself better in a Ditch than in a Palace, and so he passed this Judgment upon him : that since he would not be persuaded to come out of his House upon that occasion, he should never stir abroad again from that Day forward without his House upon his head.

This, as may be seen at once, is the Olympian aspect not only of the house, but of the garden as well. We mortals do carry our Homes with us, breathing a closer, less free air than the air of Olympus, when the reigning monarch has merely to take a toy in the head to enter into a state of matrimony. We, tortoise-like, are bound and tied by a thousand pleasant associations to our plot of earth and our patch of stars. Sooner than attend the ceremonies of the greatest, we linger by our house and in our garden, so that though we may not boast with the great world and say that we know " Dear old Jove," or " that charming wife of his, Juno," still we know that we live on the slopes of Olympus, and have a number of charming flowers for society.

203

X

EVENING RED AND MORNING GREY

YOUR old-fashioned man with a care to his garden will
look through the quarrel of his window to spy weather
signs. This quarrel, the lozenge-pane of a window
made criss-cross, shows in its narrow frame a deal of
Nature's business, day and night. For your gardener
it takes the part of club window, weather glass and eye
hole onto his world. Through it day and night he
reviews the sky and the trees, the wind, the moon
and the stars. When he rises betimes there's the sky
for him to read. When he returns for his tea there
in the pane is the sunset framed. When he goes to
bed the moon rides past and the friendly stars twinkle.

No man is asked his opinion of the weather so much
as the gardener, except, may be, the shepherd ; both
men having, as it were, a Professorship in weather
given to them by the Public. It is they who have
given rise to, or even, perhaps, invented the rhymes by
which they go.

> Evening red and morning grey,
> Send the traveller on his way ;
> But evening grey and morning red,
> Send the traveller wet to bed.

There is a verse full of ripe experience. The evening sun glows red through the lozenge-panes and into
the cottage, lights up with sparks of crimson fire the
silver lustre ornaments, makes the furniture shine again,

204

gives the brass candlesticks a finger lick of fire, shines
ruddy on the tablecloth, and flashes back a friendly
scarlet message from the square of looking-glass. On
the deep window ledge stand a row of ruddled flower
pots in which fine geraniums grow, behind them a tidy
muslin curtain stretches across the window on a tape,
on the sides of the window are hung a photograph or
two, an almanac, and a picture cut from a seed catalogue, above hangs a canary in a small cage. Only
the narrowest slip of window is clear, not more than
one clear pane, and it is through this that the evening
sun streams into the cottage room. In the morning
when our friend rises, if he finds the room flooded
with a clear grey light, a light matching the silver lustre
jugs, then he quotes his verse, to be sure, and passing his
neighbour says, " A fine day, to-day."

2

A rainbow in the morning
Is the shepherd's warning
But a rainbow at night
Is the shepherd's delight.

That sign is for the shepherd and the traveller by
night, since no ordinary being is expected to watch for
rainbows by night to the detriment of his night's rest
and his morning temper. But the shepherd must keep
a keen eye to such signs, and marks, day and night, all
the little movements of Nature, to learn her whims. As
for instance, the signs of bad weather to come :

1

That swallows will fly low and swiftly when the upper air is
charged with moisture for then insects fly low also.

2

That the cricket will sing sharply.

THE CHARM OF GARDENS

This last, of course, in wet countries, for in dry places, as in meadows under southern mountains, there is a perfect orchestra of rasping crickets in the grass But in the north, on the most silent and golden days, they say that the chirrup of a cricket foretells rain. Just as they say :

3

As hedgehogs do foresee evening storms
So wise men are for fortune still prepared.

This they say, because the story runs that a hedgehog builds a nest with the opening made to face the mildest quarter thereabout, and the back to the most prevalent wind.

Again, and this a sign everybody knows :

4

That distant hills look near.

As indeed they do before rain, and many times one hears—" such a place is too clear to-day "—or, " One can see such a land much too well," and this means near rain.

Like the swallows so do rooks change their flight before rain, and so, also, do plover, for it is noticed :

5

That rooks will glide low on the wind, and drop quickly. And plover fly in shape almost as a kite and will not rise high, one or two of the flock being posted sentinels at the tail of the kite formation.

Then, if the shepherd is near to a dew-pit, or any water meadow, or passing by a roadside ditch he will notice :

6

That toads will walk out across the road. And frogs will

change colour before a storm, losing their bright green and turning to a dun brown.

To all of these signs with their significance of coming rain your shepherd will give a proper prominence in his mind, marking one, and then searching for another until he is certain. His first clue on any hilly ground is :

7

That sheep will not wander into the uplands but keep browsing in the plain.

Having taken note of this he turns to plants, particularly to his own weather glass, the Scarlet Pimpernel, as he sees :

8

That the Pimpernel closes her eye. That the down will fly from off the dandelion, the colts-foot, and from thistles though there be no wind.

Of night signs there are many, but chiefly :

9

That glowworms shine very bright.

10

That the new moon with the old moon in her lap comes before rain.

11

That if the rainbow comes at night
Then the rain is gone quite.

12

Near bur, far rain.

This of the bur, or halo, to be seen at times about the moon.

For a last thing they say :

207

THE CHARM OF GARDENS

13

On Candlemas Day if the sun shines clear,
The shepherd had rather see his wife on the bier.

*   *   *   *   *

Our friend, the weather-wise gardener,—and, by the way, there is the unkind saying :

Weatherwise, foolish otherwise—

has several things in his neighbourhood to tell him of coming rain, as :

1

That heliotrope and marigold flowers close their petals.

2

That ducks will make a loud and insistent quacking.

3

That—so they say—the cat will sit by the fire and clean her whiskers.

4

That the tables and chairs will creak.

5

That dogs will eat grass.

6

That moles will heave.

In the garden he too will observe the birds, more especially that pert friend to all gardeners, the robin. For they say :

If the robin sings in the bush
Then the weather will be coarse ;
But if the robin sings in the barn
Then the weather will be warm.

EVENING RED AND MORNING GREY

I must confess that I have not found this come true of robins, any more than I have found waterwag-tails coming on the lawn to be a harbinger of rain, or that thrushes eat more snails than worms in the dry season. Of this last I get enjoyment enough, for there is a stone in my garden to which the fat thrushes come dragging snails. They give them a mighty heave, and down come the snails, " crack " on the stone, until the shell is burst asunder and the delicious morsel is down Master Thrush's gullet in the twinkling of an eye. The thrush is certainly my favourite garden bird, both for his looks and his song, and the blackbird I like least, for they are bundles of nerves, screaming away at the slightest suggestion of danger. The robin is a fine impudent fellow and friendly in a truly greedy way, following the smallest suggestion of digging with an eye for a good dinner, so that if you are only pulling the earth up in weeding you will have the brisk little gentleman at your elbow, head cocked on one side, and an eye of the greatest intelligence sharply fixed on you. Pigeons I regard as an absolute nuisance, their voices sentimental to a degree, in this way quite at variance with their selfish, greedy and destructive characters. So they say :

> If the pigeons go a benting
> Then the farmers lie lamenting.

Starlings are very handsome birds but as they live in congregations, or like regiments, one can have no personal feeling for them, though I love to watch them on winter evenings when they come in thousands from the fields and fly to their roosting place, making the air rustle with the quick beat of their wings.

The bullfinch is a gardener's enemy, for he will strip the fruit buds from a tree out of pure wantonness, and yet he is a brave bird and nice to see about.

209

THE CHARM OF GARDENS

All the small birds give one joy though they be robbers or enemies to young plants, or bee eaters like the blue-tit, or strawberry robbers, or drainpipe chokers like the house-sparrows, or murderers of the summer peace like the woodpecker with his quick insistent " tap, tap."

In royal and fine gardens, of course, one must have two birds ; the peacock and the owl, for these two give all the air of romance needful, though I have never myself regarded the peacock as a King of birds, for he makes too much of a show of himself, and his wife is a humble creature. I feel, rather, that he is a courtier strutting up and down waiting the King's pleasure ; a place-seeker, one who will cheer the side that pays. As for the owl, that dusky guardian of secrets, he is a far more solid and trustworthy fellow than the gay peacock, and though he snores in the day-time, his great round yellow eyes are open at the least sound in his haunt.

This is far afield from the weather, so let us give the remaining saying of birds that the gardener may notice.

> November ice that bears a duck
> Brings a winter of slush and muck.

That I hold to be very true.

There are still one or two rhymes that should be well noted, three of the rain.

1

> When it rains before seven
> It will cease before eleven.

2

> March dry, good rye
> April wet, good wheat.

210

EVENING RED AND MORNING GREY

3

> If the ash before the oak
> Then we are in for a soak.
> But if the oak before the ash
> We shall get off with a splash.

Then they say :

> Between twelve and two
> You'll see what the day will do.

And again :

> Cut your thistles before St. John
> You will have two to every one.

And,

> The grass that grows in Janiveer
> Grows no more all the year.

And also :

That flower seeds sown on Palm Sunday will come up double.

* * * * *

These are all very well, and what with one thing
and another will come true, at least as true as the
rhyme that says :

> A mackerel sky
> Is very wet, or very dry.

Still it is really to the wind that the gardener looks
most, and if he have a weathercock in his garden (which
with a sundial, a rain gauge, and an outside thermo-
meter he should always have) he will note each turn of
the wind. If he has no weathercock then he will read
the wind by the smoke of chimneys, or the turn of the
leaves of trees.

And, after regarding the wind, he may remember this :

> When it rains with the wind in the east,
> It rains for twenty four hours at least.

THE CHARM OF GARDENS

And this also :

> When the wind is in the south,
> 'Tis in the rain's mouth ;
> When the wind is in the east
> 'Tis neither good for man nor beast.

This weather lore is naturally gleaned out of many years, some of the sayings being of real antiquity, others, perhaps, newly coined, though I fancy not. In spite of them you will find every gardener has a different manner of reading the sky and the wind, some having it that mares-tails in the sky come after great storms, others that they are the portent of a gale. Some, if asked will reply to a question on the weather :

" With these frostises o' nights, and the wind veered roun' apint west, and taking into consideration the time o' year, and the bad harvest "—then follows a long look into the heavens—" I don't say but what er won't rain, but then again, I dunno, perhaps come the breeze keeps off, us mighten have quite a tidy drop." This you are at liberty to translate which way you choose, since the advice is generally followed by a portentous wink, or, at least, some motion of an eyelid curiously like it.

XI

GARDEN PROMISES

It is Winter, and when it is winter the earth is very secret, but it lies like pie-crust promises waiting to be broken. A little graveyard of the tombs of seeds and bulbs spreads before one's eyes. Each tomb has a nice headstone of white with the name of the buried life below written upon it. The virtues of the buried are not written in so many words, but their names suffice for that. In my imagination I see my graveyard like this :

HERE LIES BURIED

A

ROSE COLOURED TULIP
WHO CAME ACROSS THE SEAS
FROM THE KINGDOM

OF

HOLLAND

UNDER THIS EARTH
SHE
AND ONE HUNDRED OF HER SISTERS
ARE WAITING FOR THE SPRING
WHEN THEY WILL UNFOLD THEMSELVES
FROM THEIR LONG SLEEP AND ADORN
WITH THEIR PLEASANT FACES THE SOUTH
BORDER FACING THE STUDY WINDOW

That I see most clearly written over the spot where I tucked the hundred and one beautiful sisters in their bed of rich brown earth, and I am looking for the

213

time when the graveyard shall begin to be green with
the shafts of their first leaves. Besides these, there
are the headsticks to the Carnations, but this patch
of the graveyard is different since the tufts of Carnation grass make long grey lines against the brown
earth. Somewhere, in each of these grey tufts, is
hidden the beautiful germ of life that is growing,
growing all the time, and the wonderful chemical process is at work there (for all the plants look so silent
and quiet), that is mixing colours and rejecting colours,
and is secreting wax, and preparing perfume. Of all
moments in a garden this is to me the most wonderful.
No glory of colour or variety of shape ; no pageant
of ripe Summer, or tender early day of Spring appeals
to me quite in the way this silent time does, when a
thousand unseen forces are at work. I have often
wondered (being quite ignorant of the chemical side
of this) what happens to that drop of fresh colour the
bee brings like a careless artist flicking a brush. Sometimes in a Carnation of pure white, one flower, or two,
will show a crimson streak—a sport, one calls it. But
more curious still is the fringe edge of the Picotee. How,
I have often asked myself, does the colour edge find
its way to its proper place ? How does the plant
manage to produce just enough of that one colour to
go round each of its flowers ? I have stood by a row
of these plants that I have just planted in some new
bed, and wondered at the amazing industry going on
within them. They are fighting disease, supplying
themselves with proper nourishment, mixing colours,
and building buds and stems. It is a regular dockyard of a place except that there is no sound. I imagine
(quite wrongly, but merely because an instinct causes
me to do so) a lot of orderly forces like little drilled
men hard at work in green-grey suits. Those who

214

work underground are not in green but are in white, but should they go above the surface they would change colour owing to contact with the light, and this is due to the presence of a matter called chlorophyll in the cells which gives plants their green colour.

The underground workers are hard at it always, getting water from the ground, and in this water are gases and minerals dissolved. The workmen send this up to those in the leaves. Those who work in the leaves are taking in supplies of carbonic acid gas from the air, and the leaves themselves are so formed as to get as much light as possible on one surface. When the light meets with the carbonic acid gas in the leaves starch is formed. This is distributed through the plant to the actual builders.

You stand over the row of Carnations all silent, all still, and yet here is this tremendous activity going on, building, distributing, selecting, rejecting. A thousand workmen making a flower.

The two sets of workers, in the roots and leaves, the one sending up water and nitrogenous matter, the other making starch, are manufacturing albumenoids for more building material. And it is more easy to think of such creatures at work since a plant, unlike an animal, has no stomach, or heart, or bloodvessels, and its food is liquid and gaseous.

Now of these marvels the greatest is that of the existence of life in the plant on exactly the same initial principles as the existence of life in man. That is the substance known as the protoplasm. It is too amazing for me, and too great a thing to be dealt with here, but, as I look at my silent dockyard, there are these protoplasms, in the cells of these plants, dividing into halves and, so to speak, nestling with fresh cells in walls of cellulose.

215

THE CHARM OF GARDENS

Think of the work actually going on beneath our eyes in the one matter of the starch factory in the plant, where the chlorophyll (the green colouring matter) separates the carbon from the carbonic acid, returns the oxygen to the air, and mingles the carbon and the oxygen and the hydrogen in the water and so makes this starch.

All this goes on when we open our windows of a morning and look out over the garden and see just a grey line of Carnations we planted over-night. The workers at the roots who are so busily engaged in sending up water, are also sending with it all those things the plant needs that they can get from the earth. Thus the water may contain iron, nitrogen, sulphur, and potash. All that goes from the roots to the leaves is called sap. This, when it comes to the leaves and all parts of the plant exposed to the light, transpires, and so keeps the plant cool.

The stem, on which the supreme work, the flower, will be born, is, in the case of our Carnations, divided into nodes and internodes, the nodes being those solid elbows one sees. It is towards the supreme work that our eyes are turned. It is part, if not chief part, of the pleasure of our vigil to look forward to the day when the first faint colour shows in the bursting bud. It is for this moment that we wait and wear out the chill of Winter. It is towards the idea of a resurrection that our thoughts, perhaps unconsciously, are fixed, to the knowledge that our garden is to be born again, fresh and new in colour, in warmth and sunshine. The very secret workings going on before our eyes, all that Heavenly workshop where none are 'prentices and all are master-hands, where the bee, and the ant, and the unseen insect in the air, go about their exact duties, give one, as Autumn declines into Winter and Winter

216

rouses into Spring, some vague conjecture of the mighty magic of the growing world, where no particle of energy is ever wasted.

Life in the Winter takes on this aspect of waiting wonderment. While the rivers are in flood, and the fields are ruled with silver lines where the ditches are full, and the Sun uses them for a mirror ; while the gulls are driven inland and follow the plough, and the starlings congregate in the open fields, we prepare our pageant of flowers against those days when the slumber of the earth is over, and the now purple hedge-rows are alive with tender green. St. Francis of Assisi impressed the very sentiment on his friars, in bidding them make scented gardens of flower-bearing herbs to remind them of Him who is called " The Lily of the Valley," and " The Flower of the World."

So goes my workshop through the winter days, while a few pale ghosts of late Roses linger on the trees, sigh-ing doubtless to themselves, like old gentlemen—" Ah, I remember this place before Autumn pulled down all the green leaves, and long before all that ground was laid out for seed plots." And all the while my Roses are growing and, could one see into the colour chambers of the trees, into those wonderful studios hidden in the tiny cells, one would see these artists at work rivalling the blush of morning, the flames of fire, the white soul of innocence, the crimson of king's robes, and the orange flush of sunset. There are men, I suppose, who know to a certain extent how the secretion of these wonderful colours is arranged ; why this or that colour runs to flush a petal to the edge, or stays to dye only the flower's heart. But it will ever be a marvel to me to see how these veins flow crimson, those hold orange, and those again hold a rich yellow. The work that creates the colour of a Pansy, that gives

to the Sweet Peas those soft tints, that shapes and
colours the trumpet flower of the Convolvulus, and
builds the long horn of the sweet-scented Eglantine,
gives one a joy to which few joys are equal, and a
feeling of security with the great unknown things by
which life is encompassed.

Looking again at the garden of promises, and thinking of it still as a graveyard with headstones, I see
one which is, to me, particularly pleasant. It is by
an old bush of lavender, the mother bush of my long
hedge ; I read it to be written like this :

HERE LIES
IMPRISONED IN THIS GREY BUSH
THE SCENT OF

LAVENDER

IT IS RENOWNED FOR A SIMPLE PURITY
A SWEET FRAGRANCE AND A SUBTLE
STRENGTH IT IS THE ODOUR OF
THE DOMESTIC VIRTUES AND THE
SYMBOLIC PERFUME OF A QUIET LIFE
RAIN
SHALL WEEP OVER THIS BUSH
SUN
SHALL GIVE IT WARM KISSES
WIND
SHALL STIR THE TALL SPIKES
UNTIL SUCH TIME AS IS REQUIRED
WHEN IT SHALL FLOWER AND SO
YIELD TO US ITS SECRET

There stands the bush all neatly tied, its venerable
head at the moment covered with a powdering of fine
snow, and round it the first sharp spears of Crocus
leaves show, and the fat buds of Snowdrops, and the
ready bud of the yellow Aconite. All the garden is
waiting, the Pea-sticks are prepared, the paths have
been cleaned, and I am waiting and watching the little

things. The trees even now are whispering that it
will soon be Spring, for all they look from a distance
like a collection of dried and pressed roots sticking up
in the air, how they are drawn in purple ink against
the sky ; but one day my eyes will see a faint haze over
them as if a little mist hung about them and was caught
in the branches, and then they will change so quietly
that it is impossible to tell quite when they began to
look like very delicate green feathers, and then they
will change so suddenly that it is a shock to one's eyes
to find them in a full flush of sticky bud and leaf, and
one says in accents of delighted surprise, " Why, the
trees are out ! "

Not every one takes pleasure in a garden during the
Winter time, many regarding it as a chill and a desolate
place in itself, and taking only an interest in the green-
houses and the Violet frames ; and few would find a
pleasure in washing flower-pots by the dozen on a
rainy day, and in putting fresh ashes on the paths, and
in banking up Celery. But to the keen gardener every
inch of work in his garden is full of interest, he realises
the daily value of each thing he does, he knows of that
great silent work that is going on so near him, and so
enjoys even the burnishing of a spade, the rolling of
lawns, and loves, as I think every one does, the surgical
work of pruning the fruit trees.

Then, when the promise is fulfilled, and the world
is full of green and colour, the wondrous alchemy of the
Winter months shows its result in the glorious painting
of the flowers of Spring and Summer.

XII

GARDEN PATHS

You can get no symbol finer than a path, no symbol is more used. Of necessity a path must begin somewhere and have a destination. Of necessity it must cross certain country, overcome obstacles, or go round them. By nature you come at new views from a path and so obtain fresh suggestions. A path entails labour, and by labour ease. It must have a purpose, and so must originate in an inspiration. And yet the man who makes a path ignores, as a rule, the high importance of his task.

It is a peculiar thing that paths made across fields, and made by the very people whose business it is to reach from point to point in the shortest possible time, are never straight. Their very irregularities reflect the nature of man more than the nature of the ground they cross.

So unmethodical is man by instinct that if he were to lay out a garden in the same frame of mind in which he crosses a field, that garden would abound in twisted, tortuous paths, beds of irregular shapes, spasmodic arrangements of trees, flowers, shrubs and vegetables, a veritable hotch-potch. To overcome that he imprisons the wanderings of his mind, divides his garden into regular shapes, and drives his paths pell-mell from point to point as straight as his eye and a line will allow him. This planning of a garden is an absorb-

220

ing joy. To come new to a fresh place untouched by any other hand and to work your will on it gives one all the delights of conquest, and the pleasant fatigue of a war in which you are bound to win. You can make your own traditions, founding them for future ages—as, for instance, you may so plant your trees as to force one view on the attention. You can emulate Rome and carry your paths straight and level. In fact, that little new world is yours to conquer.

To me a winding path offers the more alluring prospect, just as it is more pleasant to walk on a winding road where each turn opens out a fresh vista, and the coming of every hidden corner is in the way of an adventure. I have just made such a path.

To be precise my path is eighteen feet long and two feet and a quarter wide. It curves twice, really in a sort of courteous bow in avoiding a Standard Rose tree, and begins and ends in a little low step of Box; this to prevent the cinders of which it is made from mingling with gravel of the paths into which it runs.

I began it on a Monday. It is made through a Rose bed that was too wide to work properly. At about nine in the morning the gardener and I stood regarding the unconscious Rose-bed with much the same gravity as men might regard a range of hills through which a tunnel was to be drilled.

I said, " This seems the best place to make a path through the bed."

The gardener made a serpentine movement with his hand to indicate the possible curve of the path and replied, after an interval : that such a place seemed as good as any.

We then, with a certain lightening of heart after this tremendous thought, walked into the bed and surveyed it. This tree would have to be moved, and

221

that one, and these half standards shifted. Good. It should be done.

It seems that the earth requires a little ceremonial even when the merest scratch is to be made on her surface. I am sure we wheeled a barrow containing spades, a line, and sticks with some feeling of processional pride. The gardener then, having come to a stop with the barrow, spat, very solemnly on his hands. It appeared to be the exact form of vitual required. In a few minutes we had pegged a way.

I suppose a spade is the first implement of peace ever made by human kind. It is certainly the pleasantest to hold. A rake is a more dandified affair, a hoe not so well-formed. The scythe and the sickle have a store of poetry and legend about them, but the rake and the hoe contain no romantic virtues. Although the plough is the recognised implement of peace in symbolical language, it joins hands with war in that same language —" turning their swords into ploughshares "—and so loses much of its peaceful meaning, but the spade remains always the sword of the man of peace, one weapon by which he conquers the ground and makes the earth yield her fruits. For me the spade.

The gardener, having spat upon his hands regarded the earth and sky as if to mark and measure the earth and the heavens, and them to witness his first cut. The spade, lifted for a moment, drove deep into the earth. The soil, pressed by the steel, turned. A new path was begun. How long is it to last ?

There are garden paths, so commenced, have made history in their day, why not mine ? Kings, Princes, Lords, Queens, Maids of Honour, spies and honourable men have trodden garden paths, measuring their small length and discussing everything in the states of Love or Country to come to some decision. The Poppies

Tarquin slew gave their message. The Pinks that Michonis brought to Marie Antoinette grew by some garden path ; that very bunch of Pinks in which lay a note promising her safety, brought her death more near. What comedies, what tragedies, vows made and broken, kisses stolen and repented, have not had for platform just such a path as mine.

At the first hint of broken soil a robin, pert and ready, took up a position on a bare limb of Penzance Briar, and began to eye us merrily just as if he, I and the garden were all out for a day's worm hunting.

Said I, " Dick, we are out to make a garden path, incidentally to make history." For I had my idea of the "History of Paths" well at the back of my mind.

The robin replied (or as good as replied), " If it's history you're after, it's insects I'm here for, so we'll come at a bargain."

Meanwhile the gardener turned another clod.

Said the robin, " I never saw any one so slow."

Slow as we might have been we were quick enough in imagination. For one thing there was the question of edging. Tiles, bricks, box, stones, which was it to be ?

Half-way down the trench we had made, just at the acute point of the greater curve, the gardener propounded the question of the edging. He leaned on his spade, and turning to me asked if I had thought to something to edge the path with. Now my thoughts were far away from that idea and were hovering like butterflies over a vision of the Path Complete. I saw, for Springtime, a row of Daffodils nodding and yellow in the breeze. For Summer I saw Carnations gleaming richly, and the Roses all blooming. Overhead the driven sky hung out blue banners of distress as if signalling for fine weather. Plumb to earth my thoughts came.

" About something to edge with ? "

Almost before I had time to speak, he continued. I had begun with the word, " Box."

Every one knows what it is to come on the rocks in the soil of a gardener's mind. It is, as a rule, some old idea taken deep root which forms a rock of resistance. Sometimes it is a rock idea about taking Geranium cuttings, sometimes an idea about the time for pruning fruit trees or the method of pruning them, sometimes it concerns certain plants which he refuses to allow will live in the garden and so lets them die. One is never quite certain when or how the objection will arise. I had sent out a feeler for Box and I struck a rock.

" Box ! ! " he said in a voice of awe, as if the gods overhearing would be angry. " Where am I to get Box from ? And if I was to get Box, Box don't grow so high,"—he held his hand a mustard seed height from the ground—" not in ten years. It's awkward stuff, Box, to deal with. In a garden this size that needs an extra man—and plenty of work for a boy too, when all these leaves is about—growing hedges of Box or what not is not possible. Not that I have anything to say against Box, far from it. No. It looks well in some places, but if you was to ask me, sir, I think it'ud be the ruin of this Rosebed."

Said the robin to me, " The man's mad."

I answered quickly, " It was merely a sudden idea of mine."

He relapsed into silence for a moment. Then he said, " flints."

I knew it was to be a battle. I hate flints. Nasty, ugly, tiresome eyesores. Gardeners love flints just as many of them love Laurels and Ivy.

I said very rashly, " But where are we to get flints ? "

Of course I should have known that he had a cartload of flints up his sleeve. He scraped his boots, walked away, and returned with a jagged thing like one petrified decayed tooth of a mammoth. This he thrust into the ground, and then surveyed it with pride.

" That," he said, " is something like."

" Something like what ? " said I.

" A double row of these," he said, " with here and there one of a different colour would never be equalled."

I agreed with him sarcastically. " Never," said I, " would they be equalled for utter hideousness. Far be it from me," I said, " to fill the hearts of my neighbours with envy of this border."

" You don't care for them ? "

" Chuck it at him," said the robin.

" I wouldn't be seen dead in a path bordered with flints," I said.

More in sorrow than in anger he removed the offending flint, and we resumed work. The last time we had used bricks for an edging they had all cracked with the frost, so that idea was left alone. Not, of course, that all bricks crack, but the bricks about here seem to be very soft.

I asked if we had any tiles.

He knew of some tiles, a lot of them, nearly buried in the earth and covered with Moss. They were an old line running by the path inside the wall by the paddock ; the path by the rubbish heap.

" But," he said, having the rout of the flints in his mind, " it would take a man all day to dig them up, and scrape them and wash them, and then he couldn't say they would be any use when it was done. And in a garden where an extra man——"

" I will do it myself."

225

THE CHARM OF GARDENS

" Fight it out," said the robin.

More or less in silence, and really in excellent tempers, we finished the trench that was to receive the cinders and ashes.

I washed the tiles. There were exactly ninety of them required. I started to wash them in the cold water of a stable bucket, and I regarded each one as a thing of beauty as I did it. After having done forty I began to think it would be a good thing to give prisoners to do to teach them discipline. After seventy, I decided to recommend that particular form of torture to some Chinese official. By the time I had finished I felt that some medal should be struck to commemorate the event.

The gardener, at the close of that day, looked at my heap of tiles.

I said, " I have finished them."

He replied, " I was just coming to lend a hand."

To which, as I was not going to let the sun go down upon my wrath, I answered, " Thank you."

I think an ash-heap is the most desolate object I know. The dreary remains of burnt-out fires make a melancholy sight, but I remember that as a child that corner of the garden where stood the heaps of ashes and ancient rubbish was as the mines of Eldorado to me. Here, if one dug deeply enough, one found pieces of broken pottery, in themselves equal, by power of imagination, to any discovery of Roman remains. To the whitened bones I found I gave names, building from them adventures more lurid than those of Captain Kydd. To the ashes I gave gold and jewels, delving as if in a mine, sifting, with childlike seriousness, the heap of fire slack, and coming on some bright bit of glass that shone for me like a kingly diamond, I held it to the light and renewed the ardour of my soul in its gleaming rays. After all, are not pieces of broken glass

226

as beautiful as many jewels if they are self-discovered and lit by the light of joy ? That corner of the garden, hidden by shrubs, by low-growing nut trees and shaded by ancient Elms, has been for me the Forest of Arden, of Sherwood, the deeps of the Jungle, an ambush, a hiding-place, a tree covered island, each in its turn absolutely satisfying to my mind. The sun's rays shooting down through the branches have found me seated, dirty, dishevelled, but incomparably happy,—a King with an ash heap for a throne.

To an ash heap, then, I repaired on the following day, there to gather loads of cinders and slack for my garden path. Already in my mind the Roses bloomed by the path side ; the tiles, evenly set, were leaned against by blue-eyed Violas ; Carnations waved gorgeous heads at my feet.

My friend the robin was there betimes and took upon himself to sing a little song to cheer me. After that, with his bright eyes glinting, he hopped upon the bed and inspected my labours.

The gardener coming upon me glanced at the row of neatly placed tiles.

" I'm glad I thought o' they," he said.

" Hit him," the robin chirruped.

" You think they look well ? " said I.

" As soon as I thought of they tiles," he answered, " I knew I'd a thought of a grand thing."

So he took all the idea to himself, and went on solemnly pounding down the cinders with a heavy stone fastened onto a stick.

And now the path is finished, and curves smooth and sleek between the Rose trees, and answers firmly to the tread. All day long I have been planting cuttings of Violas alongside the path ; and behind them are rows of Carnations.

227

THE CHARM OF GARDENS

I wonder who will walk upon my path in a hundred years time, and if by then they, whoever they be, will think our methods of gardening very old-fashioned and odd. And I wonder if we shall seem at all quaint to people who will come after us, and if our clothes will be regarded as odd and wonderfully ugly.

Once, I remember, I saw into the past in such a vivid way that I still feel as if I were living out of my date by living now. It was on the occasion of some fête in the country which was to be held in some big gardens. Certain ladies were presiding over an entertainment that set out to represent a series of Eighteenth Century booths. The daughter of the house where I was stopping had spent time, money, and taste in getting very accurate and beautiful dresses of about 1745. They wore these, powdered their hair, and placed patches on their cheeks, and prepared baskets of lavender tied up in bundles to sell at the fair.

I saw them one morning start for the place where the fair was to be held. They came into the garden all dressed and in white caps, and they walked arm-in-arm down a path bordered with Pinks and overhung with Roses, and the sun gleamed on their flowered gowns and on their powdered hair. I could almost hear them say—" La, Mistress Barbara, but I protest it is a fine morning." There was nothing incongruous in sight, just these walking flowers passing the banks of Roses, pink as their cheeks, and the Pinks white as their powdered hair. I felt at my side for my sword, and put up my hand to my neck to smooth the fall of my lace ruffles, but, alas, nor sword nor lace was there.

In the ordering of paths such as I have written there are many ways, and some are for paths all of grass, and some for tiles, and some for flags of stone, some for gravel, and some for brick laid herring-bone ways.

Each has its proper and appointed place, as, for instance,
that flags of stone are proper by a balustrade where
are also stone jars to hold flowers and stone seats
arranged. And brick, which of all the others I most
prefer, as it is more warm to look at and helps the
garden by its rich colour, is good in intimate small gardens as well as in big, and gives a feeling of cosiness to old-
fashioned borders, and is nice near to the house, and is
good to set tubs for trees on, or tubs filled with gay
flowers. Of grass paths, in that they are soft and inviting,
I like them well enough, but they are wet underfoot after
rain and dew, and need a deal of care and trimming ; but
in such cases as small set gardens with queer-shaped beds
and low Box borders, I mean bulb gardens, to be afterwards used for carpet bedding or for a show of some one
thing, as Begonias, or Zinnias, or Carnations, they are
without equal. They should be kept very precious, and
well free of weeds, otherwise their beauty is gone and
they have a lack-lustre air, very uncomfortable. As for
gravel, it is a good thing in place where the ground is low
and moist, for it will remain dry better than anything
if it is properly rolled and well made. Often it is not
properly curved and drained, and Moss and weeds collect
at the sides, whereby your garden will seem unkempt
and dull. Indeed the garden paths are of supreme importance to the appearance of your garden, as if they be
left dirty, or covered with leaves or moss they will spoil
all the neat brightness of the flowers, and are apt to look
like an unbrushed coat on a man otherwise well dressed.
This is especially the case with broad paths and drives.
How often one has judged of a gardener by the appearance of his drive ! The first glance from the gate up the
drive will give you a fair guess at the gardener and his
methods, and you can tell at once if he be a man of decent
and tidy habits, or a man to leave odd corners dirty and

full of weeds. That last man is just such an one as will burnish up his place on the eve of a garden party, and give everything a lick and a promise, and will stand by his greenhouses with an expression on his face of an holy cherub when the visitors are being shown his stove plants. That man will be for ever complaining of overwork and will wear a face as long as a fiddle if he is asked pertinent questions of unweeded paths. " Such a work," he will say, " should be done by an extra boy. As for me, am I not by day and by night protecting the peas from the birds, and the dahlias from earwigs, and the melons from the ravages of slugs ? " And you may know from this that he is the type of man who loses grape scissors, and who leaves bast about, and mislays his trowel, and neglects to give water to your favourite plants, so that they wither and die. No. Look well that you get a man who is fond of keeping himself clean, and he will keep his paths clean, as is the case in a man I know who started a fruit garden in the country. He, it was, who showed me his men working on a Saturday afternoon at cleaning up the paths. And when I stood amazed at this he took me into the shed where the tools were kept, and there I saw spades shining like silver, and forks burnished wonderfully, and everything very orderly. I clapped my hands, and looked round still in wonder, for I marvelled to see such neatness and order in a place that is the shrine of disorder—as tool sheds, potting sheds, and the like, which are a medley of stick, earth, leafmould, old pricking-out boxes, tools, wire, and other miscellaneous objects. And I marvelled still more to see through the open door men at work—on the afternoon devoted to holiday—picking leaves from the paths, and setting the place in order.

I said, " This is well done indeed."

And he answered, that this was the secret of all good

230

gardening, pride and carefulness, and that now he had shown them the way his men were so proud of their tool-shed that they brought admiring friends to see it of a Sunday afternoon. Then I knew if there was money to be made growing fruit in England (which there is) then this man would make it (which he does).

Now this talk of paths gives one the idea that people do not here make enough of their paths, as the Japanese do, for there they are skilled in small gardens, and especially in landscape gardens on a tiny scale, making little hills and woods, and views, lakes, streams, and rock gardens in a space about the size of the average suburban garden. Then they are very choice of trees, and value the turning colour of Maples, and the droop of Wisteria, and the shape and blossom of Plum and Cherry trees as fine garden ornaments, while we grow our wonderful lawns. Our lawns, indeed, are remarked by all the world, and wherever you see the words " English Gardens " abroad you will know that the people have made a lawn and watered it, and are proud of its fat smooth surface of velvet. But we make the mistake, I think, of growing forest trees on the edge of our lawns and do not enough encourage the wonderful and beautiful varieties of flowering shrubs that there be. Above all we seem to have a passion for dank, black, lustreless Ivy, beloved only of cats, spiders and snails. I have seen many beautiful walls of stone and brick utterly destroyed and defaced by ill-growing Ivy, where the bare walls would give a fine warm background to our flowers.

The great thing in paths is to make them a little secret, leading round trees to a fresh view, and interlacing them in pretty and quaint ways, but we, a conservative people, are ill-disposed to cut new paths except in new gardens, and often leave badly designed paths for lack of a little good courage. But we are learning by degrees, and I

231

think the abominations of gardening are leaving us, such as the monkey-puzzle tree in the centre of a round bed, and the rows of half-moon beds cut by the side of our lawns and filled with Geraniums and Lobelias, and the rustic seat (horror !), and the rustic summer-house made of rough pieces of tree limbs badly nailed together (horror of horrors !). Now we know more of the way to make pergolas, and terraces, and how to build summer-houses, and the curse of the Mid-Victorian gardening is come to an end with the antimaccassar, and the wax fruit under a glass case, and the sofa with horsehair bolsters.

Of course, true gardening is the work and interest of a lifetime, like the collecting of objects of Art, and as such inspires much the same eager passion and healthy rivalry. Therefore let the setting of your collection be as perfect as possible, and those paths leading to the choice collections as fine as the velvet on which priceless enamels are laid. Indeed enamel is a happy word, for what do your flowers do but enamel the earth with their sweet colours, and in pattern, choice, and variety, will surpass all things made by man alone.

And here I take my leave of paths, that great subject that should indeed be a book to itself, for if a man sit down to think of paths he begins to follow one himself, and, starting from the cradle, ends at the grave, or, pursuing some path of history, comes into the broad high-road of all learning, or looking up and observing the stars finds a train of thought in following the path of a star. In a garden path, or from it, he may meditate all these things with right and proper circumstance of mind, for he has flowers at his feet full of the meat of good things, rare remembrancers of history, and exquisite things on which to base a philosophy ; while, as for the stars, are they not the Daisies of the Fields of Heaven ?

XIII

THE GARDENS OF THE DEAD

It is a beautiful custom that we put flowers on the graves of our dead, and is more fraught with meaning than many know, for it is as a symbol resurrection that they are so placed, inasmuch as the flower that seems to perish perishes only for a while but comes up again as beautiful, and though it die into the soil it reappears all fresh and lovely with no sign of the soil to mar its beauty. But it is more beautiful to plant the graves of those we love with flowers, as then we symbolise that they are alive in our hearts and for ever flowering in our thoughts. And the shadow of the church over them is but the shadow of the wing of sleep. All our lives, said a French King, we are learning how to die ; and when the time comes we cannot help but think of that Garden of Sleep where we must be placed along with other sleepers, there to wait.

In England it has long been a habit to plant the more melancholy trees and shrubs in churchyards, as Yew trees, Myrtle, Bay, and the evergreen Oak. In this way a sense of gloom was intended, much at variance with the Christian doctrine that proclaims a victory over death. But instead of this effect of sombreness the presence of these evergreens gives an extraordinary air of quiet peace, of something perpetually alive though at rest. Often and often I have taken my bread and cheese into a country churchyard, and have sat down on the grass and

233

leaned my back against some venerable monument, and there lunched. I take it that this is no disrespect to the dead, that the living should join company with them even to the extent of spreading crumbs of bread over their resting places. I take it that the smoke of a pipe is no sacriligeous sight in the neighbourhood of tombs ; for it is but a friendly spirit prompts it, and no violation of the repose of these dead people. No ; no more than does the distant roar of the ship's guns at practice disturb these quiet souls.

In more than one churchyard there are the stocks remaining where malefactors were placed, and so seated were they that all the good folks passing in and out of church were forced to pass, almost to touch the feet of the wrongdoers as they trod the path to the porch. One place I know in particular where the stocks remain, and a goodly Yew tree having grown thick and strong behind the seat forms a fine back to lean against. From here I have surveyed the landscape over the tops of grey old tombs, now all aslant over the heads of the sleepers. Here the squire of 1640 rests facing the Cornfields once he cut and sowed and stacked. There a lady, Christabel by name, faces the flagged walk to the stone porch. There is grass over them now, and the merriest Daisies grow, and Moss covers the laughing cherubims, and Lichen has crept into the words that set forth their marvellous number of virtues. Spring comes here just as it comes to other gardens, and the trees bud just as daintily, and the young grass is every bit as green, and the first Crocus lights his lamp, and the Dandelion flares as bravely with his crown of gold.

There are these quaint quiet churchyards over the length and breadth of England, where the dead lie so comfortably under the fresh English grass. Some are full of flowers planted by loving hands ; Roses

234

grow beside the church and shower their petals over the grey stones of the tombs, and Spring flowers have been set in the grass to nod beside the headstones sleepily. Others are bare and bleak, standing exposed to wind and weather on a hillside, with stone walls about them, and a church buffeted by every storm ; yet these are sometimes most peaceful gardens, and Ling and Gorse scent the air, and twisted Fir trees, and gnarled old Pines, all leaning over, wind-bent, stand guard over the sleepers ; bees busy in the heather, lizards green as emeralds, and the bright butterflies give the feeling of incessant life ; they give that glorious feeling that the great pulse still beats ; that Nature all alive is yet at one with the dead.

The gardener of these our dead, what a queer man is he ! What a peculiar profession he follows ! To bury is but to plant the dead that they may flower into that new life. And he is usually a humorous character, a man of well-chosen words who surveys his garden of headstones and has a word for each. He is no respecter of persons, since in the tomb all are equal, and to see him at work preparing a fresh place for burial is to think that the gravedigger's work is no melancholy task. In the heat of summer, half buried in the grave himself, he sings some old catch as he shovels up the earth. " Poor little lamb," he may say of a dead child ; " well, thee'll bide here against our Lord wants 'e."

I have seen such a man, his clothes brown with grave earth, a Daisy between his lips (something to mumble, as he does not smoke on duty), and watched his face as the lytchet gate clicks. His daughter, a flower herself, is bringing his dinner, which he eats cheerfully leaning against one side of the grave for support. This, with a thrush singing somewhere, and the wheeze of the church clock, and the frivolous screams of swifts make death a comfortable picture.

THE CHARM OF GARDENS

Here we have Nature triumphant, the Earth with her children asleep in her lap. But a monstrosity has crept into our graveyards—God's Gardens—and in place of flowers with their joy, their symbolical message of resurrection, one sees ghastly things of bead work and of wax, enclosed in hideous glass cases with a mourning card in the centre of them. This is not seemly nor decent in a place where the Earth reclaims her children, where nothing ugly should be. It is within the reach of everyone to buy fresh flowers and to renew those flowers from time to time, and they should be left, if they are placed there, to die. Away then with glass jam-jars filled with water, with bead wreaths, and all ill-taste and hideous distortion of grief, and let us have our offerings made as if to the living, for our dead live in our hearts, nor torture them with horrid and distressing objects on their graves. I would have every churchyard a garden kept by the pence of those who have laid their dead there to rest ; and I would have flowers and shrubs planted and paths made, and seats placed, so that all should be kept fair and bright.

In Switzerland, where I was once, I saw the most delightful graveyard I have ever seen. The church stood on a bluff overlooking a river, a swift running noisy river that sang songs of the mountains and of the big fields and of the bustling towns, a dashing river alive with music, loving the sound of its own voice. Above was this church and its yard, and a little below, the village. The church was low-built and old, with a wooden tower on which a cock stood guard ; and it was whitewashed, and toned by sun and rain, and a clock in the tower marked the passage of time, solemnly, "tick-tock ; tick-tock." Along the south wall outside the church was a bench, and a Wisteria over the bench, and a little jutting roof over the Wisteria. This bench, time-worn as all else was time-worn (as the wall was polished by several generations of backs), faced the graveyard. If you sat on this bench you might take a glance at a man's life there in one long look, for there was a mill near by, and an Inn, and a shoemaker's, and a forge—the blacksmith was the undertaker, too, any one could see from the fact that he was making a coffin. Besides these you could see mountains covered with snow and wreathed in clouds ; great stretches of country, a wood, and the river. What more can there be, saving only a sight of the sea ?

But what struck me most forcibly was the appearance of the graveyard, for each grave had flowers growing by it, and a little weeping willow planted to hang over it, and there was something so pleasant to me in this that I was filled with delight of the place as I sat there. It was a real garden, so fresh and bright with flowers and with ugly bead-wreaths as are so usual in foreign countries, and now, alas ! in our own. And it was so homely to think of the elders of that place who sat looking at the graves and meditating—very likely—on the spot where they themselves would lie. I remembered then, as I sat there, the description of the graveyard in David Copperfield, and the words came almost exact into my head.

" One Sunday night my mother reads to Peggotty and me in there, how Lazarus was raised from the dead. And I am so frightened that they are afterwards obliged to take me out of bed, and show me the quiet churchyard out of the bedroom window, with the dead all lying in their graves at rest, below the solemn moon.

" There is nothing half so green that I know anywhere as the grass of that churchyard ; nothing half so shady as its trees ; nothing half so quiet as its tombstones. The sheep are feeding there, when I kneel up, early in the morning, in my little bed in a closet within my mother's room, to look out at it ; and I see the red light shining on the sun-dial, and think within myself, ' Is the sun-dial glad, I wonder, that it can tell the time again ? ' "

Even as I remembered those words I looked up and noticed a sun-dial on the wall of the church just over my head, and, curiously enough, just that peace that those words give to me seemed to come to me from the sight of the sun-dial, and the repose of the scene before me.

It is good, I think, to meditate on these things, and all who garden, who are, as it were, in touch with the soil, must sometimes let their thoughts linger over the other gardens where the dead are, and where Spring comes as blithely as in any other spot.

Although the gardens that are what are called " show-places," tended and nursed by a staff of men, do not bring one into such close contact with earth as earth, still in the greater garden is a peace no other place knows but the graveyard. This is no morbid thought, nor over introspective, but, I think, makes me feel more sanely and not so fearfully of death. In the same way do the poor keep their grave clothes ready and neat in a drawer, with pennies sewn up in linen to put over their tired eyes, and everything decent for the putting away of their bodies. So does the wood of trees enclose them, and good and polished wood in the shape of coffin-stools is there to bear them up. And I have heard many talk of how they wished to lie facing the porch of the church ; and others who wished they might be near by the gate so that folks passing in and out might remember them.

This may seem a subject not quite fitted to a book which is to tell of the Charm of Gardens, and yet I am sure lovers of gardens will know just what I mean. To think of and know of the peace and beauty of certain graveyards is to gain consolation and quietude such as the knowledge and thought of all beauty gives. What a wonderful thing it is that we can paint the earth with flowers, set here crimson, and there orange, here purple, and there blue; range our colours from white to cream, to deep cream, to all the shades of all the colours, to deep impenetrable purple, more black than black, like the dusky eyes of anemonies.

When it is night, and " the dead all lying in their graves at rest, below the solemn moon," the thousand thousand Daisies of the fields have closed their eyes, and the Buttercups' golden glaze is mellowed by the moonlight, still there are flowers gay in the sunshine somewhere in the world. Though the garden is chequered in the blue-green light and heavy shadows, and the owls hoot in their melancholy voices, still there are birds somewhere in the world singing. And though, across the way behind the wall, white in the moonlight, lies the dark churchyard, and all is very still there, still, I think, they, whose names are carved there on the stones, are not in the dark, and do not know the damp and mouldy earth, but are somewhere in some world more light and beautiful than this.

The solemnity of this type of thought is seldom given to me by flowers; it is more the breath of trees, and the deep places of a wood, that gives one this feeling of hush and peace. Flowers are gay, stately, exuberant, simple, but always joyous, as witness the pert questioning faces of Pansies, and the languorous droop of Roses, the stately propriety of Lilies, the romantic splendour of purple Clematis, and the passionate beauty of the coloured Anemonies. In a garden are all moods, from that given by a school of white Pinks, to the masterly exactitude of the Red-Hot Poker, or the limpid and very virginal appearance of Lavender. Youth itself comes in full blood with the blossom on fruit trees; the slim elegance of childhood with the Narcissus and the Daffodil. Daintiness herself is in Columbine; maidenly virtue is in

239

the hang-head Snowdrop. Zinnias have the melodious colours of the East ; Jasmine and Honeysuckle hold the spirit of the porch. Sweet Peas, all laughing and chattering, are like a bevy of young girls ; while the proud Hyacinth, erect up his stem, his hair tight curled, his breath strong and sweet, is to me like some hero of the days of William of Orange, a hero in a curled full-bottomed wig. The Iris has the poetry of river banks ; the Sunflower peering over a cottage garden wall, spells rustic ease. Fuschias I count very Victorian, like ladies in crinolines ; Geraniums also are prim and most polite. Wallflowers I place as gipsy-like, a scent somehow of the wind on the road ; while the Snapdragons have a military spirit and grow in brightly uniformed regiments. Carnations are courtiers, elegant, superbly dressed, yet with a refinement all their own ; and Larkspurs, like charity schools of children, all dressed alike and out for a walk, on the tall stalk. Primulas, deep-coloured or pale, I feel somehow to be the flowers of memory ; and Sweet Sultans are like Scots lords in foreign clothes. There are a hundred others, all with some little fanciful meaning to those who grow them, but all, I think, are full of joy ; no flower is sad. It is the trees, the voices whispering in whose leaves bring deeper thoughts.

There are those who say that happiness would come could we but find the Blue Rose ; and others that there are places one must need find like El Dorado ; and others that a magic charm will bring us the joy we desire. They are all wrong. Happiness lies in the Rose at your hand, El Dorado is at your door, the magic charm !—listen, there is a thrush singing.

THE END

DATE DUE
